Parastey

2001

The Book of
LUSTLEIGH
Portrait of a Dartmoor Parish

Compiled by
JOE CROWDY

HALSGROVE

First published in Great Britain in 2001

Frontispiece photograph: *Dorothy Bartlett with baskets for sale on Lustleigh Green, September, 1913.*

British Library Cataloguing-in-Publication Data
A CIP record for this title is available from the British Library

ISBN 1 84114 107 0

HALSGROVE
PUBLISHING, MEDIA AND DISTRIBUTION

Halsgrove House
Lower Moor Way
Tiverton, Devon EX16 6SS
Tel: 01884 243242
Fax: 01884 243325
email: sales@halsgrove.com
website: www.halsgrove.com

Printed and bound in Great Britain by Bookcraft Ltd., Midsomer Norton.

Whilst every care has been taken to ensure the accuracy of the information contained in this book, the author disclaims responsibility for any mistakes which may have inadvertently been included.

CONTENTS

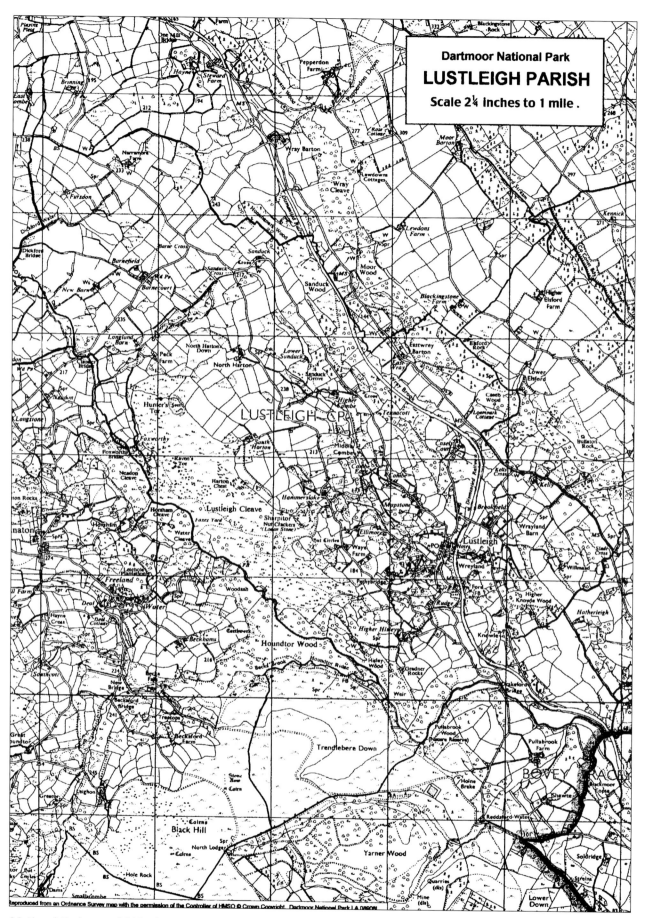

National Park map, 2000, showing the parish boundaries. (Scale 2.25 ins to 1 mile)
(Courtesy Dartmoor National Park)

AUTHORS & CONTRIBUTORS

Patrick Barker (The Lustleigh Millennium Year)
A Master Mariner, Patrick, together with his wife Alex and family of two, moved to Lustleigh in 1994 becoming involved in many village activities and organisations. Redundancy in early 2000 enabled him to give of his time and effort to the millennium activities, prior to taking a position as an independent marine consultant.

Belinda Baudouy (Lustleigh May Day)
Born 1953 in Hong Kong, Belinda is the youngest daughter of a British Colonial Crown Agent. Educated at Stover School and South Devon Technical College, she was married in 1976 to Alain Baudouy. After ten years in the Middle East, having been widowed while in Egypt, she returned to live in Lustleigh with her daughter Louise and son James. She helped with Lustleigh Sunday School for several years, joined the May Day Committee in 1990 and has been Chairman for the past six years. She enjoys many interests, friends and two dogs.

Elliot Bialick (Millennium Photographic Project)
With the sale of Elliot's marketing company and his wife Cindy's retirement from investment banking, the family travelled for two years with their young children in a motor caravan throughout the USA. Returning in 1992 to live at Higher Combe in Lustleigh, they spent three years substantially rebuilding the house, and planting 9000 deciduous trees. Elliot has rediscovered an early interest in photography and is working on a contemporary picture archive of Lustleigh people.

Margaret and Myles Bowen (Geology & Natural History/Lustleigh Horticultural Society)
Myles and Margaret Bowen lived abroad in West Africa, South America and the Netherlands while Myles pursued his career as an oil exploration geologist. Previously he had worked in Borneo after studying at Oxford and Edinburgh universities; latterly he directed oil and gas exploration in the North Sea for some 15 years for which efforts he was awarded the OBE in 1977. His most successful discovery was the Brent Field, the largest in the UK sector. Margaret and Myles moved to Lustleigh in 1992 and live at Rudge. They have three daughters.

Sandro Bullock-Webster (Roman Catholic Chapel)
Born and educated in Victoria, British Columbia, Sandro was commissioned into the Royal Marines in 1938, served at sea during the Second World War and afterwards in the Commandos. He subsequently went to sea once again before retiring at his own request to Higher Hisley in Lustleigh whence for eight years he worked in the wine trade. He owns properties in France, Somerset, Tiverton and Dartmouth and manages all of these in conjunction with Higher Hisley. He married in 1942 and has one son and five grandchildren.

Jeff Cushman (Ash Houses In & Around Lustleigh)
A Cambridge graduate in Natural Sciences (Geology and Chemistry), Jeff worked mainly in the petrochemical industry and retired to Lustleigh in 1986 to discover he was living in part of the oldest building there and next to the late Ted Robinson [qv], a very enthusiastic and knowledgeable local historian. Ted not only involved him in the Lustleigh Society, whose Secretary he became for seven years, but also activated his interest in local history. He is now President of the Lustleigh Society.

Barbara Cutts and Jean Green (Lustleigh Baptist Church)
'Our first association with Lustleigh was in 1964, when we were obliged to come to the chapel on a Sunday rota from Bovey Baptist Church because Barbara was on the Diaconate! Five years later, in response to an urgent appeal, we undertook oversight of the Youth Club that had been started by the young people

themselves on Saturday evenings in the Village Hall. As we wanted to be part of the village this led us to purchase 'Sunnymount Cottage' in 1971 where we spent 28 very happy years as Lustleigh residents.'

John Dray (The Home Guard/Growing up in the Thirties)
John came to live in Lustleigh in 1931 and attended the village school until 1939. He served in the Army during the Second World War for four years, leaving the countryside to live in London in 1956. He returned in 1981 and served on the Parish Council for eight years. His hobbies are bee-keeping, gardening, walking on the moor and studying the history of the First and Second World Wars. He is married to Grace, who is also a very keen gardener and moor walker. The couple live in retirement at Mametz, Mapstone Hill.

Tony Firth (Maps)
A professional engineer and a member of the Committee of the Lustleigh Society, Tony retired from the Midlands to the outskirts of the village in 1995.

Barry Goff (Lustleigh Cricket Club)
Barry Goff has lived at Boundary Cottage in Lustleigh since January 1999 but his association with the village spans 20 years. Throughout this period he has been a police officer at Moretonhampstead and also Lustleigh's 'village bobby'. He has played cricket for the village for ten years and has been the club's Secretary for seven of these. He also compiles somewhat haphazard contributions about the progress of the club for the edification of *Parish Magazine* readers.

Hugh Gould (Some memories of Lustleigh School)
'I spent much of my childhood in Lustleigh. My father and mother had to leave Siam before the outbreak of the Second World War. They came home with me to Lustleigh, because this is where my grandfather had lived. They built Long Close in one of my uncle's fields. My father and his brother farmed Lower Hisley together, producing flowers (dispatched from Lustleigh Station for the London market) and vegetables during the war years. I returned with my family in 1987 and bought the house that had been the Old School. I wanted my son to grow up in this beautiful place.'

Veronica Hughes (The Church House/The Old Vestry/Parson Davy)
Born in 1918 at Drewsteignton, the younger daughter of the rector, the Revd A.R.W. Peek, Veronica graduated as a teacher, MRST, in 1942. She married Doctor Mark Hughes, MD, in 1950 and they had one son. The couple retired to Lustleigh in 1976, and since then Veronica has been interested in the Parish Church and its choir, family, social and local history. She is a classical music enthusiast.

Barbara Igra (The Houses of Lustleigh)
Barbara has been an active member of the Lustleigh Society since moving to the village in 1991. She is interested in buildings, especially those used as homes, and the social history connected with them, although she stresses that she is very much an amateur in this field.

Bill Jackson (Lustleigh Show)
Bill came to Little Knowle, Lustleigh, in 1977, having moved from Bristol following his appointment as Regional Manager with a national television company. In 1986 he started his own business, 'Classic Vision'. This supports a common view that moving to Lustleigh is the killer of ambition! However, it is one move he has never regretted. An enthusiastic helper with many village events, he served on the May Day Committee for six years (of which he was Chairman for three), was a member of the Village Hall and Children's Christmas Party committees in the 1980s, and more recently has become Chairman of the Lustleigh Show.

Audrey Jenkins (Lustleigh Parish Council/Women's Institute)
Audrey Jenkins came to Underwood, Lustleigh, in 1985 with her late husband Reginald, a West-Country man, after careers in Nigeria and living for some time at Lindridge near Newton Abbot. She was formerly a committee member and President of Lustleigh Women's Institute and a committee member and Chairman of Lustleigh Horticultural Society. At the time of writing, she is President of the Newton Abbot and Teignbridge Volunteer Bureau, Chairman of the Devon Branch of Women's Corona Worldwide and the Chairman of Lustleigh Parish Council.

Ann Jones (Estates & Families/The Cleave Hotel/Farming Through the Centuries)
Ann Jones returned to the place where her parents had retired to establish a pony stud with her twin sister

after many years working professionally with ponies. The Hisley Dartmoors are now renowned throughout the world having set many records, especially at the Breed Society's own show. Ann lives at one of the oldest farms in Lustleigh and has been a committee member of the Lustleigh Society for several years.

Christopher Jones (Royal British Legion)
Christopher was born in Lustleigh in 1960, his grandparents having come to the village in the 1920s. Although now resident in Bovey Tracey since 1996, he has retained his many links with the village. An accountant by profession, he has been a member of the Lustleigh Parochial Church Council since 1979 and Treasurer of the Lustleigh Branch of the Royal British Legion since 1990.

John Lloyd (The Church Tower)
Born in Birmingham in 1920, John served in the Army from 1940–46. He was married to Joan in 1947, moved to Bovey Tracey with two children in 1969, and to Lustleigh in 1978. He served for 12 years on the Village Hall Committee and that of the Lustleigh Society (Treasurer). He has been Captain of the Bell-ringers for the last 14 years.

Hugo Pellew (The Fabric of Lustleigh Society/Lustleigh Cleave)
Hugo came to Waye Farm in 1965 and is now a Vice President of the Lustleigh Society. He is the author of *The Story of Waye in the Manor of Lustleigh.*

Janet Power, in collaboration with Jennie Powys (The Drama Group)
Janet Power, a long-serving teacher at Bovey Tracey Primary School, came to live at 'Well Park', Lustleigh, with her husband and family of four, in 1982. Secretary of Lustleigh Drama Group at the time of writing, she has both acted with and directed those actors with whom she has enjoyed much good company.

Jennie Powys, in collaboration with Janet Power (The Drama Group)
Jennie Powys (AKA Mary Powys and Jennie Powys-Lybbe) graduated from Bristol University and taught drama at Queen Elizabeth School, Crediton, before coming to Lustleigh. Later she trained and worked for ten years as a psychotherapist specialising in work with the dying. Returning to Lustleigh she was Parish Clerk for two years before a cancer operation and early retirement. She recovered and cared for her mother who died at home aged 95. She was married for eight years and had one son, Christopher, who was killed in a car crash in 1985 at the age of 20.

Alec N.E. Prowse (The Gospel Hall)
After service in the 1st Battalion Devonshire Regiment during and just after the Second World War, Alec worked for eight years on National Milk Records with the Milk Marketing Board, then for 33 years at the Heathercombe Brake School for Delicate and Physically Handicapped Children in Manaton, where he now lives in retirement.

Ted Robinson (1907–1999) (The History & Architecture of the Parish Church)
Ted came to Lustleigh in 1956 and from the first was involved in many aspects of village life, but closest to his heart was the Lustleigh Society, of which he was both a founder member and later President, as well as a frequent presenter of learned papers on parish history. He made a point of always describing the society as 'the most prestigious society in Lustleigh'. His posthumous contributions to this book are culled from his many articles in the pages of the *Parish Magazine* which covered such varied subjects as ecclesiastical history and architecture as well as 'the 89 varieties of wild plants found on Mapstone Hill'.

Jan Rowe (The Railway/Lustleigh Mills)
Jan Rowe moved to Lustleigh Mills in 1976 with her husband and two daughters. Her interest in the history of their house, a former corn mill, and of the parish in general, led her to join the newly-formed Lustleigh Society. Over the years she has moved from Secretary to Archivist and, more recently, to Vice President.

Fiona Sutcliffe Maynard (Cecil Torr & Yonder Wreyland)
Fiona Sutcliffe Maynard is a 'jack of all trades – mother of one' (Georgina Elisabeth, conceived and christened in Lustleigh). 'I have been tasked to write about my philanthropic predecessor, Cecil Torr, and our house Yonder Wreyland. As a member of the cricket, horticultural and drama societies in the village, I claim only to have contributed significantly to the last. As a Christian I attend St John's infrequently, and am an occasional organist and flower arranger. I belong to the Wolsey Lodge Association, am a keen musician, and a law undergraduate at Exeter University.'

Nick Walter (Mining in the Lustleigh Area)
Nick was born at Bovey Tracey, then lived at Forder Gardens, between Bovey and Lustleigh. After a career in the Royal Air Force, he returned to Devon and now lives at Chudleigh. He has a lifelong interest in industrial archaeology and local history, especially mining. An archivist for the Kelly Mine Preservation Society, he is also a member of the Dartmoor Tinworking Research Group. He is always happy to receive or give out information on local mines and mining families.

Bobby and Helen Wood (Restoration of the Old Vestry)
Bobby and Helen retired to Lustleigh in 1982 where they enlarged their house, Criddaford, and created a fine landscaped garden within its 7½ acres. Bobby, an international architect with a head office in London, and Helen, a director of physical therapy, both served in the Royal Air Force during the Second World War.

A specially commissioned aerial view of the village from Tony Firth.

ACKNOWLEDGEMENTS

The preliminaries to this volume cannot be complete without mention of the numerous helpers and friends who have, from their own vast knowledge of local events, given me such valuable assistance over the past year of information gathering. My particular gratitude is extended to Joan Ellis (whose accuracy in identifying schoolchildren as far back as the early 1930s is truly astonishing), Edna Franklin, Douglas Germon, David Morecombe and Bill Squires, all of whom have freely regaled me with stories and valuable information about Lustleigh in past times.

It could be said, by way of criticism of the book, that nearly all the writing has been done by in-comers to the village. While it is undoubtedly true that few of the writers are indigenous Lustleigh inhabitants, it has to be said that this has occurred not from a policy of positive discrimination but merely reflects the way in which authors have come forward to volunteer their services. It is sad to record that some of the old village family names – Amery, Bowden, Bunclarke, Wills – have not perhaps received the mention or credit that is their due, but the error, if indeed it be one, is of omission rather than commission.

Although not himself an author, special mention should be made of the map maker, Tony Firth. He has worked wonders to reproduce the 1837 Tithe Map and has successfully adapted the Dartmoor National Park map to show the present parish boundaries.

My particular thanks go to those who have lent photographs for use in this book – more than can be used. It is astonishing what a wealth of pictorial history lies hidden in family albums. It is my hope that bringing some of them into the public eye will encourage more people to make such records, and to make sure that dates and captions – unimportant though they may seem at the time – are always included. To the takers of photographs I am particularly indebted, and chief amongst these I thank Jennifer Firth for her help and skill; an example of her versatility was demonstrated when, from the dim recesses of a dusty volume in the Devon Record Office, she captured a faithful likeness of the self-effacing Parson Davy.

Lastly I record my very grateful thanks to Sarah Vantreen whose tireless, rapid and accurate typing has rescued me from the tedium of transcribing sometimes near illegible scripts into my own inaccurate and halting two-fingered typescript.

Joe Crowdy
Pepperdon Mine, Lustleigh, 2001

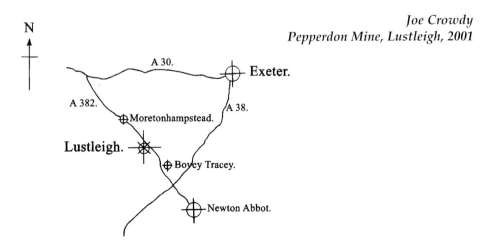

Location of Lustleigh.

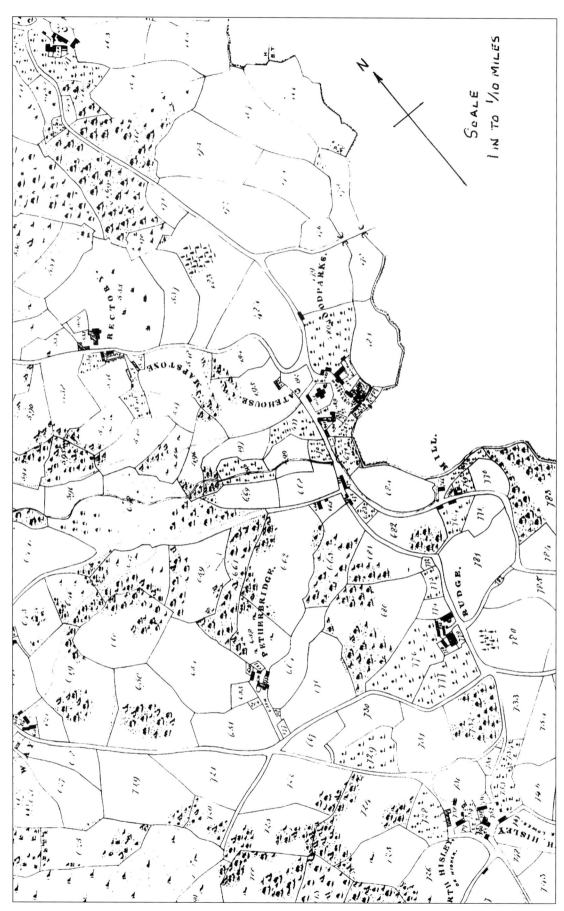

The centre of the village as shown on the 1837 Tithe Map, before the railway (Scale 1 in. to 0.1 mile).

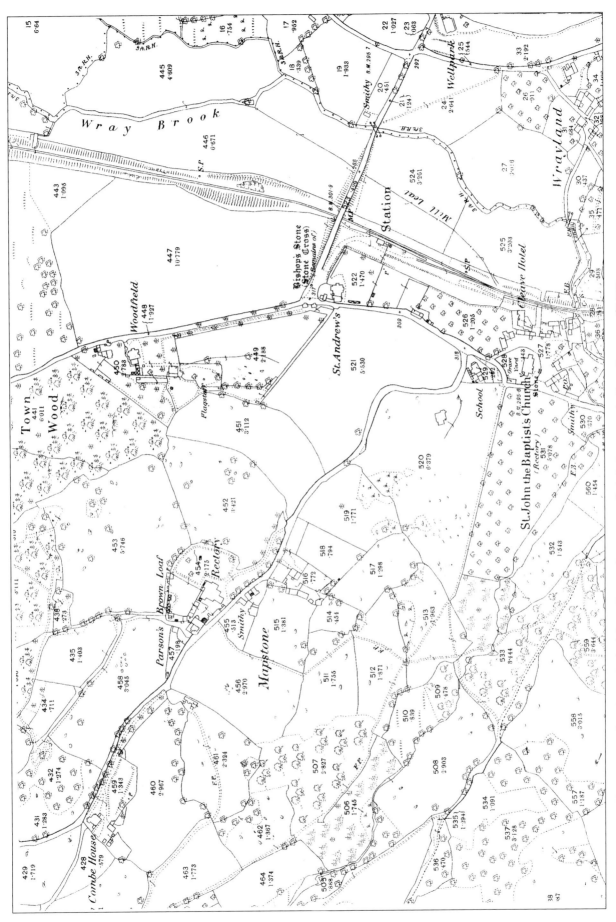

The centre of the village, 1886, after the arrival of the railway, shown on a slightly larger scale than the map of 1837.

View of Lustleigh with the church centre stage looking south-east. The roof of the Village Hall can be seen bottom left.

Brookfield, Lustleigh, looking south-east. Brookfield became part of Lustleigh in 1957.

INTRODUCTION

by the compiler, Joe Crowdy

Where is Lustleigh and why should it have a book? The village lies on the eastern fringe of Dartmoor, not on the road to anywhere but tucked away almost a mile west of the main, but narrow and tortuous, road (A382) which connects Bovey Tracey to Moretonhampstead. The reasons for the book will emerge from the pages that follow and it is hoped that readers will agree with the enthusiasts who have pioneered its production that it has been a worthwhile venture.

From as far back as 1998 the Lustleigh Society had fostered the idea of writing a history of the village but nothing much more than pious aspirations stemmed from this initiative until member Tim Hall arranged liaison and sponsorship with Halsgrove of Tiverton. The concept of an academic and erudite historical research volume was replaced by the more practical proposal of compiling a book about all aspects of Lustleigh, to be written by the people of the village for the people of the village; and that is what the present volume sets out to be. Its gestation has been prolonged by practical difficulties; Tim Hall, after an enthusiastic start, found the demands of editorship incompatible with his increasing work commitments. At an agonising meeting of the Lustleigh Society's committee he put forward his resignation and, at the same time, expressed the fervent wish that a volunteer should come forward to take on the task of compiling what had already come to be known as *The Book of Lustleigh*. There was no rush of volunteers; finally and very reluctantly the Chairman – your present scribe – agreed to become the compiler and to gather together the many threads of village history, life and activity, already mapped out by Tim, and weld the numerous potential contributions into a coherent whole. The result, a year and more later, is now before you and awaits your verdict. And by way of a bonus, the delay in publication has made a virtue of necessity in enabling a report on the second millennium festivities to be included in this volume.

In the sense that a book's theme implies some form of narrative, there is none; at worst this collection of disparate contributions from a multitude of authors could be classed – in the words of W.S. Gilbert – as a 'thing of shreds and patches'; at best it could be called a miscellany of vignettes, anecdotes and essays which reflect the coherence and continuity of community life in a lively and vibrant village. The attempt has been made to encompass not only something of the history of the village but also to bring together some sense of the very many and diverse activities which take place in a small rural community. Above all it has been written about the village, for the village and by the village. The chapter arrangement, originally intended to follow a roughly chronological pattern, has been adjusted to a more functional classification, reflecting the rather arbitrary approach to village life and customs. Reading these pages the reader will realise that much has changed since the village first assumed an identity in early-medieval times. But what has not changed is the strong sense of belonging that welds the community into a homogeneous whole. Whether this will continue into the years ahead it is difficult to say but optimism prevails; already the minutes of the Village Millennium 2000 Committee have been lodged in the Village Archives Room ready for consultation on the next occasion – the year 2999!

THE PARISH OF LUSTLEIGH

The bald census figures for the village, which recorded a population of 404 in 1891, had grown to 614 in 1991, must be interpreted with caution. In the century between these two dates the boundaries of the village have been redrawn and the present area is a great deal larger than that of 1891. Study of the 1837 Tithe Map shows that the southern boundary of the village was formed by the Wrey Brook and that the hamlets of Kelly, Brookfield, Wreyland and Knowle were excluded; they were not brought within the Lustleigh boundaries until 1957. Today's boundaries are shown in the reproduction of the Dartmoor National Park map (*see page 4*). In the Archives Room of the Old Vestry a commemorative card bears the following message: 'This card commemorates the Beating of the Bounds to mark the extension of Lustleigh Parish Saturday 11 May 1957.' The ceremony of beating the bounds, which had fallen into desuetude before that date has since then been a regular quinquennial feature and there are individuals about today in the village who can recall being forcibly reminded of the rituals of the ancient ceremony. It would be possible to dwell for some time on the confusing and differing practices of the ecclesiastical and civil boundary authorities; the church, for example, brought Wreyland and Brookfield into the ecclesiastical parish of Lustleigh as early as 1928, but it is sufficient to state, and cut a long story short, that both authorities now agree on a uniform configuration for the parish.

AUTHORS, CONTRIBUTORS & HELPERS

The variety and number of authors – there are nearly 30 altogether – reflect the make-up of the village community. To say that I am grateful to them would be an understatement, for without them no book would have been possible. Now that their writing has finally arrived on the pages of this volume I hope they will forgive me for the constant cajoling which was needed to extract contributions from some of the more laggardly. I have felt it important that every chapter – each with its own set of authors – should stand on its own. There has been no attempt to force an overall homogeneity on style or scope and readers will, I hope, find that the many variations in expression and turn of phrase create a refreshing impression. An inevitable result of this editorial policy of laissez-faire has been a certain measure of overlap and replication. You are asked to accept this occasional duplication as a necessary outcome of the need for each chapter's individual self sufficiency. Individuality is also expressed in variations in spelling that abound, an irregularity the more grammatical readers may ponder over. The phonetic approach remains strong in Devon and who knows whether the brook that flows through the village should be Wray or Wrey? Such homophones are plentiful on these pages; some Bunclarkes have an 'e', others don't; some combes have one 'o', others two; should the lane running north from Lustleigh be Casely or Caseley? We will never know for sure.

Joe Crowdy
Pepperdon Mine, Lustleigh, 2001

The village centre towards the end of the 19th century, looking across the Green. The church steps at the left were constructed to commemorate Queen Victoria's Jubilee in 1887.

A view of Lustleigh from the south with the church in the centre.

Cottages at the foot of the Green by the start of Wreyland path; the Mill Leat can be seen bottom right.

The Bishop's Stone at the ancient entrance (i.e. before 1957) to the village; it commemorates a visit paid by a medieval Bishop of Exeter.

Wreyland Manor (right), one of the oldest houses in the village, which at the time of the photograph (c.1890) was divided into three cottages and known as Hall House.

❧ *Chapter 1* ❧

AN HISTORICAL OVERVIEW

GEOLOGY & NATURAL HISTORY
by Myles Bowen

'Lustleigh is all hill, valley and rock.' Thus wrote the Revd Polwehle in his *History of Devonshire* published in 1806. The valleys and the hills reflect the underlying geology as do the plants to be found growing upon them. Underlying virtually the whole of the Dartmoor National Park is a huge mass of granite which, some 260 million years ago, was squeezed up as molten magma from beneath older (mostly Carboniferous) sedimentary rocks. These shales and limestones have almost all been eroded away by the action of rain, wind and frost to leave the bare granite tors as we see them today with numerous boulders, known as 'clitter', strewn down their sides. Along the edges of the granite mass the older sediments have been altered by heat to form, amongst other rocks, the marbles of Ashburton and the hornfels to be seen at Yarner and on Trendlebere Down. Mineralisation by fluids and vapours emanating from the granite has produced recoverable deposits of many metals, minerals and china clay. These deposits are generally to be found around the periphery of the granite and along nearby faults.

Through the north-east edge of the granite runs the great Lustleigh–Sticklepath Fault System which stretches from the Bristol Channel north of Lundy Island to the Bovey Basin and runs through our parish where there are two parallel tear, or strike-slip faults. Strike-slip faults, of which Great Glen Fault in Scotland and the San Andreas in California are well-known examples, displace the land on each side horizontally and consequently tend to run in straight lines. At Lustleigh one of these faults runs along the course of the Wray Brook towards Moretonhampstead, while the more important one follows the Bovey River valley; together these have displaced the rocks on the north-east side towards the south-east, extending along a stretch some three miles long.

Streams and rivers tend to occur along fault lines where the underlying rocks are weakest and these have given a strong NW–SE grain to the Lustleigh countryside; a prime example of this being the classic fault scarp of Lustleigh Cleave overhanging the valley of the River Bovey which follows the main Lustleigh–Sticklepath Fault.

Most of the parish is underlain by granite, but to the south of Rudge older rocks, hornfels and intrusive dolerites, occur in a highly complex faulted area. There is also an outlier of quite recent rocks (Woolley grits, similar to the eocene/oligocene sediments of the Bovey Basin) which outcrop between Knowle Wood and Kelly Farm, although they are largely covered by recent alluvium.

Mineralisation has occurred near the more northerly of the strike-slip faults and deposits of micaceous haematite were worked at Pepperdon, Kelly and Plumley Mines. This 'shining ore' is black and platelike and was originally used as 'pounce' for drying ink and latterly as a base for protective paints, as used on Brunel's Saltash Bridge. Tin was worked at Peck, near the River Bovey, and may have been smelted at the 'tin blowinge mill called Caseleigh Smitha' near the original Church House which was given to the parish in 1613. Neither remains, but traces of foundations of the 'Smitha' and of a leat can be seen on private land at Wrey Cottage. Several tin and copper shafts can be seen in Yarner Wood just outside the parish. Also just outside our boundary was a source of tourmaline, now lost, which supplied specimens to many mineral collections in the UK and overseas.

The most recent major geological event was the Ice Age which lasted for some quarter of a million years and finished only some 10 000 years ago. In fact, it was not one event, but several, with warm interglacial periods in between, with the sea level rising and falling by several hundred feet as the climate changed. The great ice sheets covering northern Europe never quite reached Devon, stopping short in the Bristol Channel but when they finally melted the water flows would have been very strong, scouring out channels and rolling huge rocks along the river courses.

The hill fields of Lustleigh have a multitude of boulders and rocks in them. Some of these are part of the underlying granite and have been exposed by erosion but others have rolled or slid downhill or been washed along by the extreme weather conditions when the ice sheets were melting. Cecil Torr speculates in *Small Talk at Wreyland* on the possible effect of an earthquake on these boulders which might be dislodged and roll again

17

(*Vol. II, p.65*). This is unlikely, but not impossible as movements can always occur along old fault lines; much less likely is the reactivation of the Lustleigh volcano! Torr also chronicles (*Vol. I, p.64*) the consternation caused to one local by a visiting geologist who came on a field trip with some students in 1906 and was lecturing them about an extinct volcano. He said it could become active again with even greater vigour. The local listened and thought it hardly worth his while to go on putting in potatoes near such a dangerous place, but asked, 'When will that hill be a-bustin forth?' The geologist then said, 'of course 30 000 years is but a moment in geological time', so the old man went on planting his potatoes! The site of this putative volcano is probably Knowle Hill where the geological map shows an outcrop of dolerite in the middle of the older sedimentary rocks of which the hill is composed.

The geology of this part of the parish is complex, but as there is nothing exceptional about the presence of dolerites in the older rocks of the area, we must regretfully abandon any claim to harbour a new Mt Etna in the parish!

The steep hills and valleys around Lustleigh provide an environment which, with its variety of habitats, is a naturalist's delight. The area is extensively wooded, with everything from small spinneys to virtual forest. Apart from a few fir and larch plantations the predominant tree is the oak along with ash, hazel, wychelm, birch and – along the streams and rivers – alder.

Fields are small and mostly permanent pasture, the ever-present granite boulders rendering any other form of cultivation difficult. Consequently, at least compared to the majority of the English countryside, ours has changed very little over the past half century. This must be to the benefit of wildlife, which must also be favoured by the amount of moorland and rough pasture, notably on Lustleigh Cleave.

As in most of Devon we have no shortage of wild flowers, with snowdrops in the New Year being followed by abundant primroses and bluebells, the latter being particularly beautiful in the woods along the River Bovey valley. The banks of our narrow lanes in early summer, being unsprayed, are a delight to the botanically inclined walker, if not to the motorist. In summer butterflies abound and rarer species such as the brown hairstreak, the white admiral and even possibly the purple emperor may be seen.

On the ground there is a thriving badger population, their well-used tracks being seen in every field and hedgerow. Foxes enjoy a degree of protection (which poultry owners no doubt deplore) as the hunt never comes to Lustleigh while otters are present in both the Wrey Brook and the River Bovey having returned recently after an absence of many years. Deer are also to be seen by those prepared to get up very early with roe being the most common, but also fallow and very recently arrived the muntjac. All cause significant damage in gardens and plantations. At the smaller end of the mammalian scale the woods lining the Bovey Valley provide a sanctuary for the now rare dormouse.

In late summer the cries of young buzzards demanding food from their parents is a common, even irritating noise. Buzzards are very common here, as indeed throughout the West Country. If they are commonly seen they are possibly outnumbered by the tawny owls whose presence in every wood only becomes obvious at night. Less often seen but also well represented are sparrow hawks as some local pigeon fanciers know to their cost. Rarer, but occasionally seen, are raven, merlin, hobby, peregrine falcon and heron among the larger birds. Sadly the barn owl, once abundant here, is now rarely if ever seen, and this despite the relatively unchanged habitats referred to above. Of smaller birds all three woodpeckers are represented, while kingfishers and dippers occur on the larger streams and rivers. Blackcaps, redstarts and pied flycatchers (the last mainly at nearby Yarner Wood) may also be spotted.

Lustleigh from the south; the railway line crosses from left to right.

ESTATES & FAMILIES
by Ann Jones

Lustleigh is situated on the eastern fringe of Dartmoor, a village with a history which goes back well before Domesday. There are the remains of stone hut circles close to one of the most regularly used paths on the Cleave to the west of the village and just a few hundred metres from one of the oldest farmhouses in the area. The Manor of Lustleigh was in existence well before the great gathering of information about the country of England which went to make up the Domesday Book in 1086, and the lord of the manor paid tax on the amount of land he owned there.

The name Lustleigh does not appear in Domesday but several experts consider that Lustleigh Manor is recorded as Sutreworde or Sutreworda, Anglo Saxon for 'South of the Wood'. In Domesday the lord of the manor was Ansgar who had held it from the time of King Edward the Confessor who died in 1065. Ansgar had taken on the manor from Walter, a man shrouded in mystery as only his name has come down through time. The Manor of Sutreworde, or Lustleigh, comprised some 1200 acres under cultivation divided into about 12 farms, plus a large area of forest. The largest farm of roughly 200 acres belonged to the lord of the manor, while the rest averaged about 70 to 80 acres each. In addition there were five swine herds which grazed the forest whose herdsmen had to give their lord 61 pigs a year, and five bee-keepers who paid the lord seven 'measures' or 'sestiers' of honey a year. Bee-keeping is apparently not often mentioned in Domesday so it must have been considered an important part of the local income in this case. There were probably about 155 men, women and children living in and around Lustleigh at the end of the 11th century.

Lustleigh continued to be part of a large estate right up to the beginning of the 19th century when it was finally broken up. The line of ownership of the Lustleigh Manor estate many centuries ago has become rather hazy though certain people have been identified from time to time. Two centuries on from Ansgar, around 1260, Sir Wilham de Widworthy was the owner. There is speculation that the effigies in the north wall of Lustleigh Church of a knight and a lady are those of Sir Wilham and his wife, though others feel that these are of Sir Robert Dinham and his wife Emma, née Widworthy.

Across the Wrey Brook lies a part of the village which only officially joined the parish of Lustleigh about 50 years ago. This portion of the village is known as Wreyland and during the 15th century the lords of the manor of Wreyland were three John Dynhams in succession, though whether they were relatives of the Lustleigh Dinhams of two centuries before is not clear.

About 100 years after the Manor of Lustleigh was in Sir William de Widworthy's hands it passed to William Burleston at the end of the 14th century, and then quickly on to Sir John Wadham in 1403. For the next 200 years it remained with the Wadham family who were well known both in Devon and as holders of high office in England. Sir John was Justice of the Common Pleas and his son became High Sheriff of Devon in 1430. In turn his son Sir Nicholas was Vice Admiral and Captain of the Isle of Wight. Sir Nicholas's grandson, Nicholas, was a very wealthy man and he and his wife Dorothy founded Wadham College, Oxford. After his death in 1609 the manor passed to his heirs, his three sisters, as Nicholas and Dorothy had no children. All three sisters had married but all had died before their brother so the one third inheritance of each was duly passed to their children.

The eldest sister Florence had married Sir John Wyndham, head of a famous family related to no less than four of Henry VIII's queens, Jane Seymour, Catherine Howard, Anne Boleyn and Katherine Parr, as well as to the great Protector, Somerset. Two Wyndhams were Vice Admirals in the 16th century, while later Wyndhams held high ministerial posts during the reigns of George I and George II. Florence's third of the Manor of Lustleigh passed to her son Sir John Wyndham and much of it stayed in the family for the next 200 years.

The second sister Joan was the wife of Sir Giles Strangways of Melbury in Dorset. They were also a well-known family and the forbears of the Earls of Ilchester. Joan's son John inherited her third of the Manor of Lustleigh, but this had been sold by the end of the 17th century. The youngest sister Margaret had married Nicholas Martin of Athelhampton and they only had four daughters, so these each inherited one-twelfth of the Manor of Lustleigh. In those days estates were not divided up physically into three equal shares, but each heir would own one third of every farm, cottage and quit rent in the manor as shown in the old deeds using the term 'an undivided one third of the manor'. So in fact every farm, etc. in the Manor of Lustleigh had no less than six landlords after 1609!

Meanwhile, fairly early in the 15th century, the Wills family made its appearance in Lustleigh, or at least in the neighbouring hamlet of Wreyland across the Wrey Brook which used to divide the two close communities. There John Willmead was a tenant of Willmead Farm in Wreyland in 1447, but it was not until his great-great-grandson Henry, who lived a century later, that their surname became Wyll. Interestingly, Henry's brother John used Wills, but as spelling in those days tended to be phonetic the difference was understandable.

From then on the family proliferated. Henry's son Richard, himself one of four brothers, had six sons of his own, and most of them moved across the

19

Left: *The four younger sons of John and Elizabeth Wills of Higher Hisley in 1904.*

Left: *John Wills of Higher Hisley.*

Below: *Elizabeth Wills of Higher Hisley.*

Higher Hisley in 1910.

Wrey Brook into Lustleigh. Despite their father having died when they were young, by middle age the eldest son George was prosperous enough to buy three-twelfths of no less than three farms in Lustleigh, leaving a younger brother Henry at Willmead Farm. George carried on the family tradition with seven sons. Though one died young the rest as they grew up spread further afield, becoming tenants of five farms in Lustleigh, one in Ilsington (see *The Book of Ilsington*) and possibly one in Bickington. They were obviously good farmers and widely recognised as such locally. Son George also believed in buying in more parts of his farms whenever possible, acquiring a further five-twelfths of Rudge and Lower and Higher Hisley in two deals, one before and one after his father's death in 1663.

By now it had become customary in the Wills family to name their first three sons George, John and Thomas, though which name was used for the eldest depended on which brother was the father, the eldest son always taking his father's name. This has bedevilled many trying to trace the various members of the Wills family. During one period in the middle of the 18th century there were no less than five George Wills, four John Wills and five Thomas Wills, all closely related, around at the same time in one small village!

At the end of the 18th century John Wills, second son of Thomas of East Wrey, saw his younger daughter Joanna marry Francis Daniel, a young man reputed to be an illegitimate son of the Duke of Clarence, later King William IV. John is said to have given his daughter a dowry of her weight in gold! Whatever the facts the young couple lived in the

grandest house in the district and proceeded to have the largest family in the area, no less than 20 children evenly divided into 10 of each, between 1798 and 1823. Joanna's elder sister Elizabeth never married, but was wealthy enough despite the large dowry given to her younger sister to be able to buy in two farms and part of a third when the Wyndham estate in Lustleigh was finally sold in 1805. Around the same time another Joanna, daughter of George Wills of Rudge and so a second cousin of John Wills, married her cousin John Wills of Smallacombe Farm in Ilsington. One of her grandsons was William John Wills who, with his partner Burke, became the famous explorers of the heart of Australia and their names are revered in that continent to this day.

In the middle of the 17th century another family with a name which was to become well known not only locally but also nationally in the 20th century, arrived in Lustleigh. Nicholas Amery of Bridford married Honor Worthilake of Middle Coombe Farm where her father was the tenant. In 1670 their son Nicholas was named as the last of the extra 'lives' added to the tenancy agreement for the farm, and for the next 200 years Middle Coombe stayed with the family. The Amery family did well and 100 years later various Amerys were taxed in seven different places around the village according to the Land Tax Assessments for 1780, a total of £12.3s.8½d. At this time the Wills family was still well ahead of the Amerys as their tax was £22.18s.2d. for 13 places. However, over the next 28 years the Amery family doubled the places they were taxed on while the Wills reduced theirs by one, so that their relative positions were reversed.

East Wrey in 1890.

The 19th century saw many changes in Lustleigh. In the early 1800s the last of the leases of the farms and houses owned by the Wyndham estate were sold, mainly to the sitting tenants. The Wills and the Amery families took full advantage and bought in 20 different places between them. But not all had their forebears' ability to farm well and prosper, while others were starting to look elsewhere for their living as opportunities opened up in the wider world. In the 1820s another family bought property in Lustleigh and several descendants are still living in the village today. John Gould of Taunton was the first to become interested in the area though he never actually lived in the parish. He bought three properties, Boveycombe, Lower Hisley and Knowle, which his descendants retained for many years before moving to other places around the village.

Lower Hisley was acquired from George Wills and his mother. This farm had been finally bought from the Wyndhams at the beginning of the 19th century by Roger who quickly handed it on to his son George some time after the latter's marriage. But George unhappily was not like the rest of his fore-bears and seemed to go through money like water. He must have been a rather charming man as he always seemed to find someone else to borrow from as soon as this was required, though some quickly saw through him and demanded their loans back almost immediately. George died in 1827 still owing money, and leaving a wife and young family, the eldest being George, aged 21. To clear their father's debts they sold Lower Hisley to the man who had bought the small farm below theirs, Boveycombe, a few years earlier. Young George was in the true family mould of good farmers and not only stayed on

farming Lower Hisley but later farmed at Knowle as well for the Gould family. This led to him being buried from Knowle, while his tombstone claims him to be 'of Lower Hisley'.

Soon after the middle of the century the railway to Moretonhampstead was built up the Lustleigh Valley on land owned by Thomas Wills who was also a director of the company. Thomas' family owned much of the centre of the village as well at that time, including Gatehouse Farm which is now the pub, The Cleave. They also owned East Wrey Farm on the main road between Bovey Tracey and Moretonhampstead, which has been an hotel since the mid-20th century. Towards the end of the 19th century Thomas Wills of the East Wrey family became a solicitor and his younger brother William took on the main road farm. Then in 1897 William sold it to another George Wills whose family came from a farm on the top of the hill behind East Wrey. This George had made his money trading in Australia and London and had retired to Pepperdon, above Moretonhampstead. After that William went to farm in Gloucestershire and founded a famous herd of pedigree Large Black pigs using Lustleigh as his herd prefix.

Around the middle of the 19th century Leopold Amery was born. Leopold's father Charles, although the eldest son, had decided that farming was not for him and left Lustleigh to join the Indian Civil Service. After marrying in London Charles and his wife Elizabeth went to India. Charles was an official in the Indian Forestry Commission when his children, Leopold, Geoffrey and Harold, were born. However, the marriage did not last as Charles committed adultery and was divorced by his wife in 1885. Leopold, an extremely clever boy, went into politics in his

The Cleave Hotel, formerly Gatehouse Farm, in the late-19th century.

*Ellimore Farm and
Lustleigh Cleave beyond.*

forties and was in turn Political Secretary to the War Cabinet when he re-drafted the Balfour Declaration, Assistant Military Secretary to Lord Derby acting as a negotiator between British Zionists and the War Office, and Dominions Secretary in the 1925–29 Baldwin Government. His next term of office in any government was in 1940 with Winston Churchill as Secretary of State for India, after Leo had made a speech quoting Oliver Cromwell which was generally considered to have brought down the Chamberlain Government. His younger son Julian was also to serve in Government after the Second World War and later became Lord Amery of Lustleigh. Both he and his father are buried in Lustleigh churchyard, and there is a handsome memorial to Leopold in the west wall of the south transept. There are other Amerys in Lustleigh to this day, relatives of those above, and one family still farms though not at the original place which is now a private house.

In the middle of the 20th century the last of the Wills-owned farms, Higher Hisley and Waye, were sold. This brought to an end the longest link, over 500 years, that any family has ever had with Lustleigh. The Wills have now nearly disappeared from the village as the last in the direct male line died in 2000. The latest of the families to have had a long association with the village,

the Goulds, have moved around Lustleigh quite a bit during the 175 years of owning property here, from their beginning in 1825 owning a small farm to the present day. Practically all the original farms are now private houses and much of the land has either been sold off or built over. Now there are only three working farms in and around the village, compared with the dozen or so right up to the end of the last century, and only one is worked by one of the old families, the Ainerys.

Thanks must go to Colonel Pellew whose 'Waye' has been very helpful, and to Miss Caroline Belam for her great assistance with research on Leopold Amery.

Waye Farm in 1952.

Family Groups

The Golden Wedding of John and Elizabeth Rice, married 24 March 1848.

Ellen Morecombe (1852–1929) with daughters Kate and Polly, and grandchild, in 1907.

Ellen Morecombe with her four surviving daughters at Coronation Terrace in 1913. Left to right: Kate (with dog), Annie, Polly (with violin) and Alice.

Family Groups

Elizabeth Wills and her family of eight boys at Higher Hisley.

An Edwardian group in the garden of the Great Hall (then the rectory).

A Belgian refugee couple, housed by public subscription at Elmfield in 1914.

LUSTLEIGH CLEAVE
by Hugo Pellew

Lustleigh Cleave has been part of Lustleigh since time immemorial. When William the Conqueror granted the Manor of Lustleigh to Ansgar the Cleave would have been part of that estate. But because of its woody, rocky and in places precipitous nature it was unsuitable for cultivation by the 'villeins' who occupied the small farms, and it was known as the 'wasteland' of the manor or the 'manorial waste'. However, despite being unsuitable for cultivation, it could provide many things useful to people of the manor, such as rough grazing for cattle, sheep and ponies, particularly in the spring (known as common of pasture), beech mast and acorns in the autumn for pigs (pannage), timber and wood for repairing fences and farmhouse buildings (estovers), peat and turf for fires (turbury), and fish from the river for the farmer's family (piscary), as well as sticks and furze for all and sundry.

The lord of the manor would grant to certain of his tenants the right to take these commodities from the Cleave and these rights were known as 'common rights'. In an early survey of the manor of 1624 a dozen farms are named as having 'common of pasture in Boveycombe Cleave': Boveycombe, Higher Hisley, Pethybridge, Waye, Ellimore, South Harton, North Harton, Peck, Higher Combe, Middle Combe, Foxworthy and Caseleigh. In those early days the Cleave was known as Boveycombe Cliffe, which is really the natural name for it. It is bounded on the north-west side by the River Bovey, 'combe' is the old name for valley, and 'cliffe' because of its cliff-like nature in some places.

There used to be a well-known Logan stone here known as the Nutcracker Rock (*see map*) until one day in 1950 some fellows from the village with crowbars tipped the upper rock off the lower rock and it plunged down the steep slope below leaving the lower rock in situ.

There is a massive rock called Harton's Chest opposite South Harton, though why it is called Harton's Chest is a mystery; but there was a man called Gilbert de Hyrton mentioned in 1332 who, almost certainly, lived at South Harton Farm. There are the remains of hut circles just at the foot of the Nutcracker hill indicating an early-Bronze-Age settlement, and another hut circle just over the boundary wall with South Harton. 'Ravens Tor' is a large rock on the cliff-side above Foxworthy and until quite recently there has always been a pair of ravens nesting in the vicinity. At the flat part towards the northern end there is the outline of an early British camp.

The owner of the Cleave was by right the lord of the manor and from 1400 to 1609 members of the Wadham family were lords of the manor at Lustleigh.

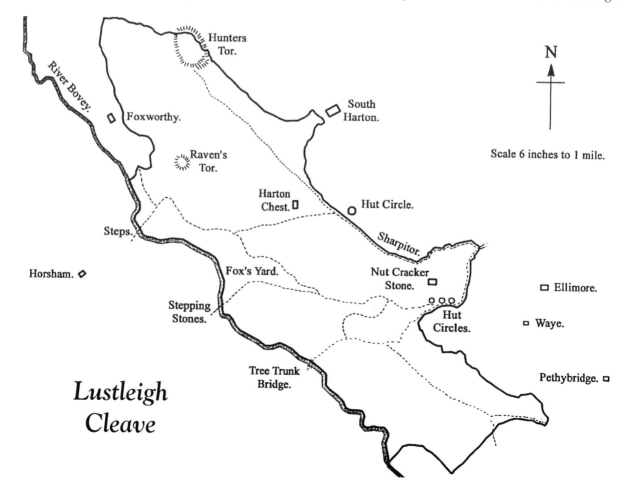

N

Scale 6 inches to 1 mile.

Lustleigh Cleave

The Logan stone known as the Nutcracker on Lustleigh Cleave before being dislodged and destroyed.

When Nicholas Wadham died in 1609 his heirs were, as previously mentioned, his three sisters, and it was the children of these three sisters who each inherited one-third of the manor, which in turn included one-third of the Cleave. Soon after Nicholas Wadham's death the ownership of the manor, including the Cleave, was divided as shown in the accompanying diagram; the Wyndhams retaining their one-third until 1805, the Strangways theirs until 1681 and the Martins' one-third becoming further divided, one-twelfth going to the Codnors (who sold their one-twelfth in 1650) and three-twelfths going to a local Lustleigh man called Richard Caseley.

The Wyndhams retained their third of the manor until 1805 when they sold their one-third of each farm and cottage to, in the majority of cases, the occupants of the same. In 1681 the Strangways had done the same thing and in 1659 the Codnors had done the same for their twelfth. But in all three cases the owners did not sell their part ownership of the Cleave.

As to what Caseley did with his three-twelfths of the Cleave, there is some confusion. He was acting in partnership with two other Lustleigh men, George Wills of Higher Hisley and Nicholas Gray of Boveycombe Farm. According to Gray, Caseley sold him the three-twelfths of the Cleave in 1630 but there is no actual deed to confirm this, and some years later Gray sold one-twelfth to Nosworthy of Foxworthy. What he did with the remaining two-twelfths is not known. However, in 1632 Richard Caseley sold to George Wills three-twelfths of the Cleave together with three-twelfths of Higher Combe Farm. This

deed exists to this day at Higher Combe. Which of these two sales by Caseley is the true one?

That is how the situation remained until the middle of the 20th century with the owner of Higher Combe claiming three-twelfths, the owner of Foxworthy one-twelfth, and a third belonging to the Wyndhams and another third to the Strangways, although neither of these two families, nor the people of Lustleigh, were aware of this. A group of local farmers with grazing rights acted as a self-appointed committee managing the Cleave.

Three events occurred, which called into question the ownership of the Cleave. The first was a well-publicised poaching case in 1886 when three men were taken to court for poaching game (i.e. rabbits) on the Cleave. The main difficulty was in ascertaining who was entitled to bring the case. Sporting rights can only be exercised legally by owners of the soil. Fortunately T.S. Amery of Higher Combe had a clear title to three-twelfths of the Cleave, by Richard Caseley's deed of 1632. Accordingly T.S. Amery and eight others brought the case to court. The case was heard at Moretonhampstead, both sides being represented by solicitors. The accused freely admitted that they were poaching but contended that as nobody could produce title to ownership of the Cleave nobody could prosecute them. Whereupon T.S. Amery produced his deed of 1632 and that broke down their defence and each of the three were fined 5s.0d. or imprisonment.

The second event which raised the question of ownership occurred when the Nutcracker Logan

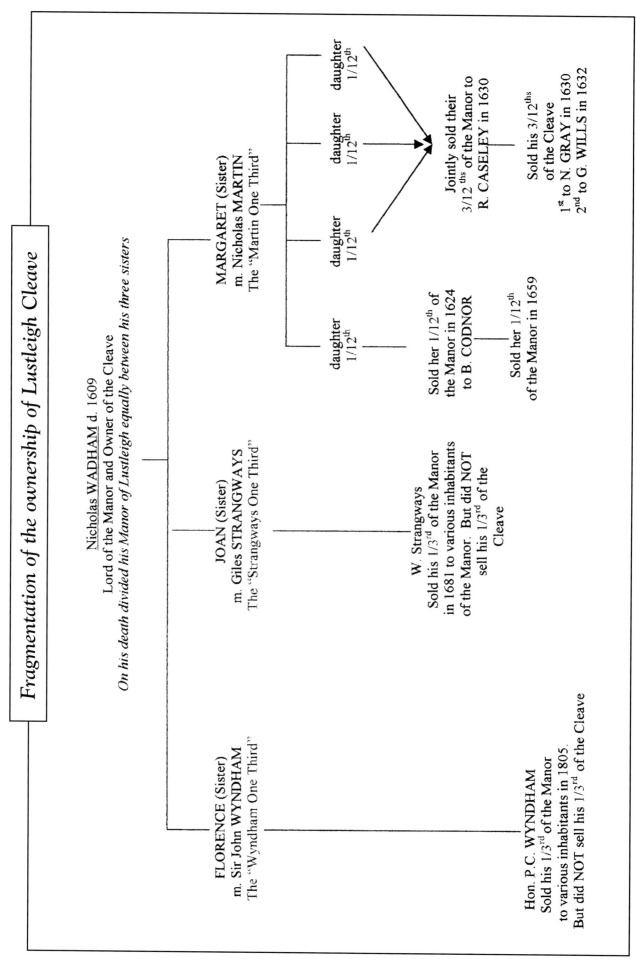

Fragmentation of the ownership of Lustleigh Cleave

Nicholas WADHAM d. 1609
Lord of the Manor and Owner of the Cleave
On his death divided his Manor of Lustleigh equally between his three sisters

FLORENCE (Sister)
m. Sir John WYNDHAM
The "Wyndham One Third"

Hon. P.C. WYNDHAM
Sold his 1/3rd of the Manor
to various inhabitants in 1805.
But did NOT sell his 1/3rd of the Cleave

JOAN (Sister)
m. Giles STRANGWAYS
The "Strangways One Third"

W. Strangways
Sold his 1/3rd of the Manor
in 1681 to various inhabitants
of the Manor. But did NOT
sell his 1/3rd of the
Cleave

MARGARET (Sister)
m. Nicholas MARTIN
The "Martin One Third"

daughter
1/12th

daughter
1/12th

daughter
1/12th

daughter
1/12th

Sold her 1/12th of
the Manor in 1624
to B. CODNOR

Sold her 1/12th
of the Manor in 1659

Jointly sold their
3/12ths of the Manor to
R. CASELEY in 1630

Sold his 3/12ths
of the Cleave
1st to N. GRAY in 1630
2nd to G. WILLS in 1632

stone was damaged by some local young men. This vandalism caused a considerable stir in the village and long discussions as to who was responsible for the work of replacing the dislodged rock. The Parish Council held an emergency meeting at which opinions varied between the National Trust and the Chairman of the Devon County Council! In the end it was agreed to ask the Army if they would come and restore the rock to its former site. A Territorial Regiment of Royal Engineers agreed to make an attempt at the task. A gantry was rigged up and the rock, weighing several tons, was being slowly raised when the tackle broke and the rock crashed down the slope, struck another rock and broke in pieces. The woody hill where the lower rock of the Logan stone still lies is known to this day as the Nutcracker. The owner of Foxworthy (Mr Hunt), who claimed ownership to one-twelfth of the Cleave, wrote to the Parish Council protesting that as an owner of the Cleave his permission should have been sought before the Army was called in, but I don't think any notice was taken of this complaint.

The third event, which decided the ownership of the Cleave, was the passing of the Commons Registration Act of 1965, under which all common land had to be registered together with the names of all those who claimed common rights over the Cleave, and finally those who claimed ownership of it. Claims for common rights were the first to be dealt with. All claims for common rights were published and objections to people's claims submitted. Claimants then had to produce documentary evidence to support their claims or withdraw them. It will be remembered that there were 12 farms named in the Manorial Survey of 1642, which were granted 'common of pasture in Bovie Combe Cliffe'. Finally all unresolved claims came before the Commons Commissioner in Exeter Crown Court and his decisions were registered with the Registration Authority in Exeter. The final phase was to resolve who were the legal owners of the Cleave. The owner of Higher Combe had an undisputed claim to three-twelfths, and the owner of Foxworthy claimed ownership to one-twelfth, although there was some doubt as to his evidence in support of this claim. These two claims covered four-twelfths, a third of the Cleave. Another third had been owned by the Strangways family when they had owned a third of the manor until 1681 when they sold to the occupants of the farms and cottages (who thus became owners of one third of their properties), but there is no documentary evidence that their one-third of the Cleave was ever sold. Similarly the Wyndham family owned one-third of the manor until 1805 when they sold, like the Strangways, to the occupants of the farms and cottages. These sales are, however, all recorded, and there is no

evidence that they sold their one third of the Cleave at the same time.

There are several possible reasons for this. Both the Wyndhams and Strangways were absentee landlords, and their agents or stewards, who made regular visits to Lustleigh, were chiefly concerned with the properties that paid rents, which would be listed in their Rent Book, but the Cleave paid no rent and would not have been in the Rent Book. The Cleave is also not visible from the village and the casual visitor would not have been aware of its existence. Whatever the reason it has to be accepted that the descendants of the Wyndhams and Strangways did not sell and therefore must still be the owners of their respective thirds of the Cleave, though completely unaware of the fact. Contact was made with Mr George Wyndham, the head of the family, and with the solicitors of the Strangways, now the Earls of Ilchester, both of whom were very surprised at the news, but agreed to submit claims of ownership of a third. In due course in 1982 the Inquiry was held and the Commons Commissioner decided that for purposes of Registration the ownership of the Cleave was rested in the Public Trustee under the Law of Property Act of 1925 but that the 'beneficial owners' were as follows:

(a) Mr C.G.D. Evans, as the owner of Foxworthy, owned one-twelfth of the Cleave and Mr M. Robertson, as the owner of Higher Combe, owned three-twelfths of the Cleave.

(b) The Holland House Trustees representing the Earls of Ilchester, descendants of the Strangways (one-third).

(c) Mr George Wyndham (one-third). However, since Mr G. Wyndham had died since the hearing and had not been able to submit some documentary evidence, which he had been asked for at the hearing, his claim had not been confirmed.

The Commons Commissioner also stated that the Public Trustee had no powers to act in the Trust unless requested by more than 50 per cent of the beneficial interest who could then appoint their own trustees in place of the Public Trustee. This decision has been registered with the Registration Authority in Exeter. And so Lustleigh Cleave, which began centuries ago as the 'wasteland' of the manor under the ownership of the lord, and which has remained much in its natural state, jointly owned by absentee lords and managed by a small committee of farmers with grazing rights (two of whom were joint part owners), has ultimately had the vexed question of who had common rights and who are the joint owners resolved and recorded.

THE FABRIC OF LUSTLEIGH SOCIETY: MEDIEVAL TIMES TO THE 19TH CENTURY

by Hugo Pellew

During the 15th and 16th centuries the most important person in the manor was the lord of that manor. Next to him came the parson (Lustleigh had a rector), appointed, paid and housed by the lord. With the exception of three farms and the Church House, which were held freehold, the lord owned all the farms and cottages which were held by rent-paying tenants. The three freehold farms, Pepperdon, Caseley and Foxworthy, together with Church House, although owned by their occupiers, did have to pay to the lord a small 'quit rent'. At that time Wrayland was a separate manor with its own lord and manor court – the boundary was the Wray Brook – but the people of Wrayland did attend Lustleigh Parish Church.

Successive members of the Wadham family had been lords of the manor here since early 1400, although they did not live in the parish. Their family seat was at Edge in Somerset near Ilchester, but their steward would visit Lustleigh two or three times a year to collect the rents and other dues, to keep his records up to date and to convene and hold the manor court where erring tenants could be dealt with. Additional duties of the steward included periodically making an inventory of the manor for his lord, which was known as a 'survey' of the manor. In this were set out the 'customs' of the manor – a list of rules governing the behaviour of the inhabitants. In a Wadham survey of Lustleigh dated 1 September 1615 the customs of the manor listed included many items, among them the custom that when the tenancy of a farm or cottage changed hands the new tenant had to pay the lord a 'heriot' which was the 'best beast' on the farm. Another was that copy holders were by custom to live on their farms, and could lease some of their land for pasture. They had to grind their corn at the mill of the manor. All disputes had to be referred to the manor court. The widow of a tenant who died while still holding the tenancy was to continue to hold the tenancy so long as she lived sole and chaste. Also referred to is the vow of 'frank pledge'.

Every man and youth above a certain age living within the boundaries of the tithing (a district containing ten householders each responsible for the behaviour of the rest; with the tithingman acting as the chief man of the tithing) had to be admitted officially to that tithing. This form of admission, which was known as 'frank pledge', was carried out as follows: the 'novice' took an oath and paid a 'pledge' or surety for his conduct; the oath was originally a Saxon oath by which the novice swore that he would neither be a thief nor the accomplice of a thief. In the reign of King Canute the novice took the oath at 12 years of age. Later the oath included loyalty to the king and the lord of the manor. The tax was known as the 'censure' and was two pence and went to the lord of the manor. The pledge or surety could be either a relation (even the father) or not a relation (such as the householder).

At the first sitting of the manor court there would be a 'view of frank pledge' to ascertain that all eligible persons had duly been admitted to the tithing – this was contained in the tithingman's report. If any person failed to report for admission, the court would order a 'distraint' on the householder concerned. If that had no effect and the novice failed to appear at the next court sitting, the householder was 'amerced' (i.e. fined) one penny and the distraint again imposed. This process was continued until the novice was eventually sworn in. A 'distraint' was a form of seizure of something that belonged to the man and the detention of it until he had complied with what was required.

The manor court would be convened by the steward on one of his periodic visits to Lustleigh at Barncourt, the capital or demesne farm of the manor. All of the copyhold tenants of the farms and cottages had to attend and absentees were fined. The court dealt with all matters of discipline and order and had powers of dealing with offenders. From the record of a meeting of the manor court of 6 May 1667 we find that the whole of the assembly was referred to as the 'homage' and that a certain number of those attending were selected as 'jurors'. The proposals put forward were known as 'presentments'. Fines for absenteeism were as follows: 'Freeholders 6d., Lease and copyholders 3d.' The presentments were as follows:

> We present the death of William Cosens who died since the last Court upon whose death there happened to the Lord for a Herriot of 20 shillings.
> We continue the presentment against Richard Dolling for suffering his house (Gatehouse; the present Lustleigh Hotel) to be in decay to be repaired by 28th September next 15sh and 4d.
> We present Peter Miller of Half Pound Cottage for the want of thatch on his house to be repaired by Michaelmas next or fined 14sh.4d.
> We present Leonard Elliott for letting his house (Hillhayes) be in decay to be repaired by Michaelmas next or fined 3sh.4d.
> We present South Hittisleigh (now Lower Hisley) for a broken down wall to be repaired by 3 May next or fined 20sh.

The court would also have had to have dealt with a number of other matters, incidents such as an 'affray' when a man named Boudon hit another, Wollecote, with a 'hanger' (a short sword curved near the point), whereupon Wollecote hit Boudon with a

View of Pound Cottage in the middle of the 19th century.
(The excavations at the rear are part of the railway construction.)

'staff', and then again with a 'hanger' (sic). Joan Merdon hit Wollecote with a muck fork, so Wollecote hit her with a 'switch'. In a separate incident John hit Comyng with a 'drill' then Comyng hit John with a stone. In both cases the parties were fined without any question of who hit the other first!

A case of burglary to be dealt with in 1481 involved one John Gille of Moretonhampstead who broke into Rolf Golde's house, maltreated him severely and carried off a horse valued at 10 shillings. John Gille never appeared to answer the offence.

'Estrays' were also dealt with at the manor courts. Any creature straying on the manor became the property of the lord of the manor unless the owner claimed it within a year and a day. To reclaim it the owner had to attend the court, give formal proof of ownership and pay 2d. for the creature's keep, and find someone to act as his security.

During the Civil War Parliament decreed that all males over the age of 18 had to sign a 'Protestation of Loyalty to the King and to the Protestant Religion'. In Lustleigh 55 male persons signed, or made their mark, and among the signatories are the names of the two constables, Gregory Whitborne of Lower Combe and Stephen Berry of Peek.

By 1600 the village constable had replaced the tithingman. Having changed from a manorial to a parish figure, he was unpaid as such but had his expenses paid out of the parish rate. He was responsible for early militia contingents and their equipment, for apprehending offenders and putting them in the village stocks and for impounding stray animals in the village pound. Pound Cottage survives to this day in the centre of the village, but the pound itself no longer exists. It is now the Village Green.

A direct descendant of the Constable Gregory Whitborne of Lower Combe whose memorial stone is in the floor of the church near the font, is living in the village – Col J. Whidbourne, but no longer at Lower Combe.

In 1805 the lord of the manor sold what interests he had in the manor and in the majority of cases it was the farmers who were the purchasers who then became owners of the whole of their farms. With the departure of the lord and the closing down of the manor court the farmers with the exception of the rector became the most influential people in the village – they were landowners, employers of labour and owners of considerable wealth. This is well illustrated by a fascinating account of a bench seat which used to stand by the wall of the church in the centre of the village. The account reads as follows:

31

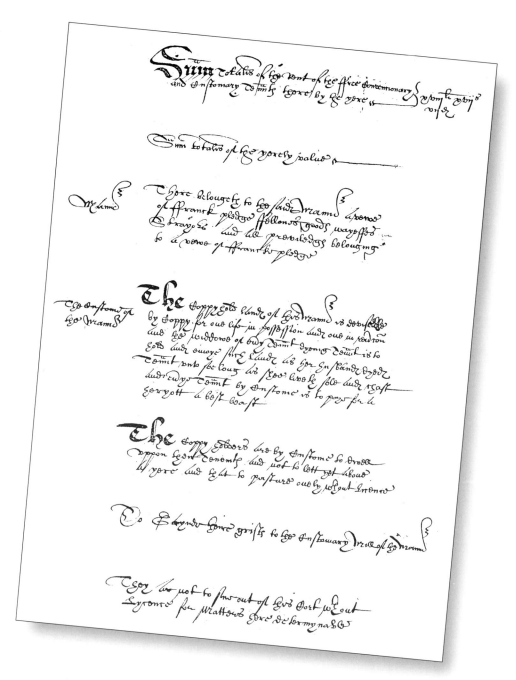

Facsimile copy of an extract from the 1615 Survey of the Customs of the Manor. It reads:

SUM totales of the Rent of the Free Convenciory and Customary Te'ments there by the yere.
Sum totales of the yearely value £18.17s.7d.

There belongeth to the said Mannor a vowe of Frank Pledge. Fellones, goods, wayeffes
and strayes and all priviledges belonging to a vowe of francke pledge.

The Customs of the Manor
THE Coppyhold lande of this Mannor is devisible of the Manor by Coppy for one life in possession and on in rev'con
and the widdowe of ev'y Tennt dyeing Tenan't is to hold and encoye such lande as her husbande dyees. Tenn't unto
soe long as she liveth sole and chast and ev'ye Tenn't by Custome is to paye for a heryott a best beast

THE Coppyholders are by Custome to dwell upon their Tenem'ts and
not to lett yet above a yere and that to pasture only without licence

To Grynde theire grists to the Customary Mill of the Mannor.

They are not to sue out of the Cort wthout Lycence for Matters here determynable.

Agreement for the Seat by the Church door 13 Oct. 1755

Be it remembered that whereas the aforesaid Seat against the South Wall of the Parish Church of Lustleigh just before the Church Door and where women have usually sat and hath and doth of Ancient right and custom from time immemorial belonged to the three Estates of South Hisley, Caseley and Eastwray in the parish of the aforesaid. And whereas the said seat was by length of time become in a very weak shattered and ruinous condition. Now this is to certifie whom it may concern that George Wills of South Hisley, Samuel Nosworthy of Caseley and Thomas Wills and George Miller of Eastwray did agree for themselves their Wives and Successors to pull down the old and to build a new seat in its place, which said new seat hath (by and with the consent and Agreement and Approbation of the Minister and Church Warden) been now lately new built and risen up by William Carnsley the whole cost and charges thereof amounted to One pound and Ten shillings whereof George Wills hath paid Ten Shillings for his third part for South Hisley Estate, Samuel Nosworthy hath paid Ten Shillings for his third part for Caseley Estate and Thomas Wills hath paid Five Shillings for a half a third part for Eastwray Estate and George Miller hath paid Five Shillings for the other half third part for Eastwray Estate. And it is further agreed by and between all the parties aforesaid that the said George Wills shall have full Liberty and Authority for to place two persons to sit in the said seat for his third part of the said seat. And the said Samuel Nosworthy shall have the same power and authority to place two persons to sit in the said seat for his third part of the said seat. And the said George Miller and Thomas Wills shall place but one person each of them to sit in the said seat for their third part of the said seat.

In Witness whereof all the parties above have hereunto set their hand this 13th Day of October 1755

The mark of
Geo Miller
Thomas Wills
Samuel Nosworthy
George Wills

The south porch near where the contentious seat (see above) was sited.

The Houses of Lustleigh

by Barbara Igra

People have lived in Lustleigh for thousands of years. There are the remains of Bronze-Age hut circles in the Cleave above Waye Farm and of an Iron-Age hillfort near Hunter's Tor. These settlements were abandoned because of a worsening climate, but better weather and increasing populations brought the Celts here. The presence of a Celtic community is inferred from the shape of the churchyard (raised and oval) and part of a Celtic gravestone which has now been moved to inside the church. There is little evidence of any Roman influence on the local Celtic farming community despite the large settlement of Isca Dumnoniorum at Exeter. In AD540 the plague reduced the Celtic population and coincided with a mass migration to Brittany.

Saxons were the local lords when the Normans conquered England. Lustleigh is Anglo-Saxon for 'the most loved place'. Although not mentioned in Domesday, Lustleigh is shown there as a demesne farm of some 200 acres (possibly Barnecourt) and with 11 or 12 villein farms averaging 70 acres each. In Lustleigh and Wreyland (also not receiving a direct mention in 1086), the farms have their roots in Domesday and the names of all but two (Boveycome and Condor) exist in some form to this day.

Very little remains of the 13th–16th-century buildings; most of the earliest surviving buildings probably do not date from any earlier than the 16th century when cob was replaced by stone. In Lustleigh, the oldest houses are thought to be the Old Hall (the rectory from 1609 to 1927), and Caseley Court. In Wreyland, the six old houses which formed the hamlet of the same name have their origins in the time the manor was split up in 1337 after John de Moules died without a male heir. These are now individually owned and are called Wreyland Manor, Bow Cottage, Souther Wreyland, Yonder Wreyland, Middle Wreyland and Lower Wreyland.

In 1919, Cecil Torr (who then owned most of Wreyland) was cutting a hole for a new window in the west wall of Bowhouse, as it was then called, and found a coin dating from the reign of Henry III, 1216–73, embodied in rock-hard cob.

Buildings have been rebuilt and altered, land added or sold, and farms divided (often for inheritance reasons). A survey of the manor in 1612 showed that apart from 23 farms scattered around the village there were buildings around the church and those that still survive include: Church House, which was once the poorhouse and is now used as an independent school; Gatehouse Farm, which is now the Cleave Inn; Staple Cottages, which were originally occupied by weavers and are now known as Stable House; and Pound Cottages, which are now residential. There were also two mills, and cottages at Hammerslake and at Hillshay were the home and workplace of a blacksmith.

Gatehouse Farm which today is the Cleave Hotel, the village pub.

Above: *The Courtyard of the Old Hall.*

Left: *The Union flag and the Royal British Legion Standard in the south-west corner of the church.*

Below: *A side view of the Old Hall.*

Cottages at the foot of Wreyland path; the tree-lined cricket field can be seen to the left behind the cottages.

Primrose Cottage, built in the late 1940s on the site of the old store where Dorothy Bartlett sold baskets.

Pound Cottage in the 1930s.

A count taken in 1642 showed 53 adult males living in Lustleigh. By the 18th century, most of Lustleigh was in the ownership of the Wills family and Wreyland was in the ownership of Nelson Beveridge Gribble, the lord of the manor, who lived at Knowle until 1797 when his son sold the property and the lordship to Francis Daniell. Gribble did retain a property called 'Yonder Wreyland' which was subsequently inherited by the Tarr family (the name later became Torr). The original house was destroyed by fire and eventually rebuilt in the 1930s after the death of Cecil Torr in 1928.

Little permanent building went on until the start of the 19th century when an Act of Parliament released the last third of the Manor of Lustleigh for sale and made it possible for farmers to acquire the freehold title to their properties. Several farmhouses were rebuilt, including Rudge and Lower Hisley. The 1837 Tithe Map and Schedules (a copy is in the village archives) showed Lustleigh as still being very much a Celtic village in terms of layout with a small centre around the church and dispersed farmsteads and hamlets for several miles around, many with the rights to graze and collect bracken and firewood on the Cleave.

The arrival of the railway line in 1866 resulted in a significant change to the village with the development of several houses, some quite substantial. Supplies for the building works were brought in by rail which also made it possible for people to live in the scenic surroundings of Lustleigh and Wreyland whilst commuting to work in Newton Abbot, Exeter and Plymouth. It became a popular retirement area, especially for those leaving the services or returning from working in the colonies. Tourists came by train to enjoy the scenery and walks in the Cleave and guest-houses and hotels were built. To quote Cecil Torr from his book *Small Talk at Wreyland*, who, in turn, quotes from what his grandfather wrote in September 1849: 'I find most people like Wreyland, that is, those advancing in years: so quiet and sheltered.' And then in January 1864:

I cannot fancy that any railway improves scenery, but this will not disturb it as one might imagine... They fancy it is cutting up the country and letting in more people, which will destroy the scenery and the quiet of the neighbourhood; but they think more of its introducing new society than destroying the scenery.

Cecil Torr himself wrote:

When the railway came, a plan was drawn up showing how the hillsides were to be laid out in the accepted Torquay style; and two such villas were built, but happily no further harm was done.

Were these Torquay villas perhaps St Andrew's and Combe Hill?

At around the turn of the century as there was no Local Authority housing and there was a shortage

St Andrew's, typical perhaps of the so-called 'Torquay villas'.

of properties available for working people to rent, the 12 terraced houses of Brookfield were built (*see page 12*). The initial builder went bankrupt after building just two of the houses and he was bought out by the grandfather, Mr Bill Squires, a resident of Lustleigh at the time of writing. His grandfather finished the development and let the houses out to miners of Kelly Mine and the other local mines as well as quarry workers and those working for the farmers or larger houses. The rent was 5 shillings a week (including rates). One house became a police house and another a bakery. The land Brookfield was built on had previously been agricultural land so its appearance on the landscape made quite a difference

to the character of the main road into Lustleigh.

In the 1920s there was another spate of building when the estate of T. Wills was broken up and houses built on fields. At the same time Cecil Torr's Wreyland estate was broken up and many of the cottages went into individual ownership. Brookfield, Wreyland and Knowle were then part of the parish of Bovey Tracey but joined Lustleigh in the boundary changes of 1956. These boundary changes have gone on throughout the centuries with land and farms being split from Lustleigh to join neighbouring parishes and vice versa.

Local Authority housing came to Pethybridge in the 1930s and again in the 1950s as did the bungalows opposite the war memorial. Primrose Cottage Tearooms, despite appearances, were built in the 1940s. Trains to Lustleigh ceased in 1956 with the 'Beeching Cuts' and the disused buildings are now a private house.

Very little house building has taken place over the past 40 years, and the majority of these are rebuilds or conversions of previous buildings. A good example of the mix of periods in Lustleigh is perhaps the lane from Bishopstone to Caseley. Until 1856 the only house on this lane was Caseley Court but it now contains 11 separate dwellings. Caseley Court, which was originally a farm but is now a private house, is one of the oldest houses in Lustleigh with origins in the 14th century. Documents, now lodged with the Devon Record Office, exist from that time. William de Caseley is listed as a taxpayer in the Devon Lay Subsidy of 1332. The other ten

Hall House, now known as Wreyland Manor.

Caseley Nursery at Bishop's Stone, built in the 1920s but now replaced.

The Cleave Hotel in years past.

properties on this road are: Caseley Close, which was converted from an old farm building; Caseley Cottage, which was built in 1897 as two cottages (probably to house workers connected with Caseley Court) but is now one home; Caseley Wood, built in 1965 on land which originally belonged to Caseley Court; Woodley House, one of the most recent houses, built in 1990 on the burnt-out stables of the adjoining property; Combe Hill, built in 1860 in what Cecil Torr called 'the Torquay villa style'; its detached stables and gatehouses, which became separate homes in 1950; Woodfield, a bungalow built in 1934; Caseley, also a bungalow built in 1932; Bishopstone, a bungalow built around 1930 which at one time was a garden nursery and tearooms, and later became the site of the coalyard; and Beechnut and Honeysuckle Cottages, originally the gatehouses to Combe Hill but sold off in 1950, which have been extended to make two homes.

The end of the 20th century saw two new houses being built fairly close to the centre of the village; one is a rebuild of a wooden bungalow and the other is on old railway land.

The quiet secluded village of 150 years ago with a population of 246 has seen a threefold increase in residents. There are now some 250 households, three churches, a school, a dairy, a Post Office, a pub, a café, and a car repairers. Although there is no actual hotel, it is also a holiday village for people staying in rented cottages or bed-and-breakfast accommodation as well as being a popular place to visit for the day.

With stringent restrictions on new development by the Planning Authority, Dartmoor National Park, it would seem unlikely that there will be much new building in the years to come. One wonders what Cecil Torr and his grandfather would now write about Lustleigh – would they approve?

The Cleave Hotel
by Ann Jones

One of many listed buildings in Lustleigh, the Cleave Hotel began as a farmhouse, Gatehouse Farm, before becoming the local pub around the middle of the 19th century. The building itself dates from around the 16th century and has several old features such as the stone slab floor of the through passage, and the bread oven on the left of the large fireplace in the bar. It was owned for about 200 years by the Wills family before it became a public house. An early landlord, Mr Woodward, who died in 1889, was a very unusual candidate for the post of landlord; an excerpt from his obituary in the *Parish Magazine* drew readers' attention to the 'striking fact that Mr Woodward was a teetotaller, and that he did much to promote temperance in drinking.'

The Cleave Hotel today.

✣ Chapter 2 ✣
CHRISTIANITY

THE HISTORY & ARCHITECTURE OF THE PARISH CHURCH
by Ted Robinson

The oval-shaped churchyard high above the surrounding ground suggests that this site was a Romano-British burial-ground. The Celtic grave-stone (Datuidoc's Stone), originally in the floor of the church porch but now in the north aisle, tends to confirm this opinion. But no doubt there have been a number of churches here since Datuidoc who is thought to have been buried between AD550 and AD600.

It is probable that the first part of the present church, a simple rectangle plus the south porch, was built about 1250, during the Early-English era of Gothic architecture; the simple lancet windows in the chancel, the double piscina and the three sedilia support this opinion.

The first addition to the church came about half a century later. The south chapel was added very early in the 14th century by the lord of the manor, Sir William le Prouse. This entailed demolishing part of the south wall and the mutilation of the east side of the porch. Sir William built it as his mortuary chapel and – for him – it was very important that he should be buried in his own chapel. Unfortunately he died while visiting his other manor in Holbeton, and before the family could do anything about it, he was buried there. This was a calamity. Sir William had no sons and so his daughter, Alice, was the heiress. She petitioned the Bishop of Exeter to have her father's body exhumed and re-buried in the Lustleigh chapel. Bishop Walter Stapledon would not allow this and soon afterwards was murdered. In addition to being Bishop of Exeter, Walter Stapledon was also Lord High Treasurer and therefore a friend of King Edward II. Half the country was up in arms against the monarch and one fateful day when Bishop Stapledon was walking down Cheapside he encountered a body of men who recognised him as a friend of the monarch. They set upon him and stabbed him to death.

Bishop Stapledon's successor was James Berkeley, an aristocrat and brother of Lord Berkeley of Berkeley Castle in Gloucestershire; he was chosen by the Exeter Chapter and consecrated in Canterbury Cathedral. Sir William's daughter Alice now petitioned him for the re-burial of her father but the new bishop, like his predecessor, would not allow it. The subsequent bishop was John Grandison and in due course Alice petitioned him. To her joyful surprise he said 'Yes'. And so, 13 years after his death, Sir William's body was brought to Lustleigh and buried in his chapel, where it lies under his effigy to this day. The document authorising the exhumation of Sir William's body was issued from the Bishop's Palace in Chudleigh, the ruined remains of which can still be seen.

Bishop Grandison lived for another 44 years devoting his time to building the nave of Exeter Cathedral. His tomb, along with those of Bishops Stapledon and Berkeley, may be seen in the

The church from the north-west.

Cathedral. During this time King Edward II was arrested by his wife, Queen Isabella, and lodged in a dungeon in Berkeley Castle where he was subsequently murdered

The next addition to the church was the tower; it incorporates a perfect specimen of a Perpendicular window, the distinctive features of which are the mullions which go in a straight line from top to bottom. It would appear that towards the end of the 15th century the population must have grown for the church was enlarged by the addition of the north aisle. This involved the destruction of the original north wall and its replacement by pillars to support the roof. The windows of the north aisle are typical of the degenerate, dying days of Gothic architecture.

The vestry is a Victorian addition in tasteful imitation of the Early-English style. There have been no further changes to the structure since then.

The Parish Church of St John the Baptist, viewed from the south-west. The clock is modern, installed in 1962.

The south porch, which bears clear evidence of the mutilation caused by the later building of the south transept (or chapel).

The nave looking east (before the installation of electric light in 1936).

Detail of the rood screen (assigned to the reign of Mary Tudor, 1553–58). The rood figures were added in 1929.

The Gould memorial lantern in the churchyard.

The altar and east window.

Candelabra and stained-glass window in the north wall of the Lady Chapel.

Datuidoc's Stone (c.AD550) in position on the west wall of the north aisle.

43

The lych-gate and steps; the latter were built to celebrate Queen Victoria's Jubilee in 1887. The tree on the left is no longer there.

The Reverend William Gordon Baillie (the rector 1904–10) undertaking his parochial duties on his horse 'The Curate'.

THE CHURCH TOWER
by John Lloyd

Lustleigh's church tower, in the heart of the village, must be the most well-known building in the parish. It features in many photographs and postcards on sale locally and is open to visitors every day from first light to dusk. Open that is, except for the bell tower itself where the granite spiral stairway to the clock chamber and above that again to the belfry has to be kept locked to safeguard both the climbers and the bells. Thus the bells which have been an integral part of the Parish Church and parish life for hundreds of years are mostly heard but rarely seen, except of course for occasional cleaning and maintenance.

However, the tail ends of the bell-ropes are to be seen at all times suspended above the ringing position on the floor of the church immediately inside the west door and directly under the belfry. The rope of each of the six bells is fed down through the floors of the belfry and clock chamber into the church.

Lustleigh's bells have called parishioners to church through the ages and they ring out each Sunday, as joyfully today as in years past. The team of ringers has also taken part with success in many competitions as is shown by some of the various illustrations included here of teams and individuals past and present.

Above: *A group of Lustleigh bell-ringers at the west door, 1930s. Left to right: George Morecombe, Tom Payne (blacksmith), Tom Cole, Sylvester Morecombe, Lewin Hill (stonemason), Mark Germon, Jacob Wright, Dick Bourne.*

Below: *Prize-winners at Buckland in the Moor, 17 July 1937. Left to right, back row: Jacob Wright, Mark Germon, George Morecombe; sitting: unknown parson (not the rector at Lustleigh), Lewin Hill, Tom Payne, Sylvester Morecombe.*

Left: William Rice (1852–1933) who was born at Cheriton Bishop and worked all his life as a carter and carrier. It was said that he could take his horse and cart from Lustleigh to Exeter and back in a day. He was a Lustleigh bell-ringer for 50 years and tower captain for 25.

Below: The ringers of the Millennium peal. Left to right, standing: Sue Connell, Brian Roach, Terry Davy, Meg Gould, David Connell; sitting: John Lloyd (captain of the bell-ringers).

Lustleigh Clergy

1262   Peter de Tautone
1310   John de Lusteleghe
1318   Peter de Honetone
1318   Hugh de Roches
1338   John de Blakedone
1341   Nickolas de Westone
1341   Richard de Brankestone
1343   John Elys
1347   William Coldoke
1349   Joel de Affatone
1349   John Affetone
1401   John Etewelle
1406   John Burleghe
1428   Ralph Cole
1460   Thomas Arture
1500   Roger Dayman
1509   John Londone
1513   John Colles
1529   Stephen Whyte
1566   Nicholas Coplestone
1607   Thomas Comyn
(1659)   Edward Basill
1698   William Hutton
1720   Joseph Shebbearn
1735   Andrew Warren
1762   Thomas Hutton
1775   William Trivett
1779   Robert Tripp
1791   John Mudge
1847   Frederic Ensor
1888   Henry Tudor
1904   William Gordon Baillie
1910   Arthur Lindsey Palmes
1914   Herbert Johnson
1926   Henry Basil Martin
1927   Robert Ryder
1945   Rupert E.G. Newman
1957   Norman McGee
1969   Edwin W.F. Deacon

The Revd Edwin Deacon was to be the last rector of Lustleigh and his retirement in 1985 ended an unbroken succession of more than 700 years. In 1986 the Revd Kenneth E. Jackson was appointed as 'Priest in charge' and his retirement in 1995 brought to an end Lustleigh's ancient tradition of a resident parson. In 1996 the Revd A.R. (Bob) Leigh was installed as rector of the newly-created United Benefice of Moretonhampstead, Manaton, North Bovey and Lustleigh, and in the year 2001 the Revd Ian Hellyer succeeded him as the rector of the United Benefice.

THE CHURCH HOUSE
by Veronica Hughes

Church houses in England belonged originally to the churchwardens and thus to the Church. Where they have been sold, they still retain part of their name to denote their origin as, for example, in 'Church House Inn'. In the past, the Church body, sometimes aided by the wealthy, took on the responsibility for the housing and education of the poor and vagrants, built almshouses and schools and set up charities to alleviate suffering. Rents from church houses were often used to this end.

During the Middle Ages a church was used for both religious and secular purposes, the sanctuary being kept strictly for morning and evening services on Sundays, but the nave then being used for secular activities and church 'ales' after the services. This situation was not without its problems and was frowned upon by the clerical hierarchy and some laity who followed the biblical teaching of Our Lord when he angrily cast the moneychangers out of the Temple, saying, 'my house is a house of prayer but you have made it a den of thieves.'

The community was thus in need of a venue where they could relax and enjoy drinking, dancing and conversation. Church houses came into being in the middle of the 15th century and were built adjoining, or close to, the church. The land was either given by the landowners or let at a peppercorn rent. The houses, including facilities for brewing and baking bread and pastry for social occasions, were built by public subscription given to the church-wardens and therefore owned by the Church. At this stage the houses were not looked after by rectors, and the churchwardens could let the buildings on condition that they could be used for church ales, particularly at Whitsuntide and other festivals. They collected the rents, which they used for repairs and maintenance of the church and to look after the poor and sick. No exact date is given for the demise of church houses but a large number ceased to be used for their original purposes from the late 16th and early 17th centuries so they did not have a long life. It seems that closure was due to lay and not clerical pressure, possibly partly because of rowdy behaviour; many were sold by the churchwardens, became schools or possibly almshouses. A large number were built in the West Country and some remain in use to this day, as in Lustleigh. Many, sadly, were demolished.

In many cases those church houses which were principally used as meeting places were often replaced by church or village halls.

Unlike most others, Lustleigh's church house is still an ecclesiastical trust administered by the Diocesan Finance Committee in the role of Custodian Trustees, and by the rector and churchwardens as managing trustees. Church House stands outside the churchyard, across the public road and to the east of the church itself. On the outside wall to the left of the porch there is a black metal plaque which declares 'The Church House, An Ancient and Historic Building.' To the right of the porch a sign tells you that the building is now Lustleigh School. Long ago in Lustleigh there appears to have been a poorhouse at Caseleigh (now Caseley – a mile north of the village) left by Thomas Nosworthie in about 1613. Nothing seems to be known of this cottage now or its site except that it was on Caseleigh land. The present Church House, probably rebuilt and much altered over the years, may have been built before 1764 to house poor people as there is no history of an almshouse in the village. At one time it may also have been used as a rectory for a celibate clergyman. New rectories were built when priests were allowed to marry and needed houses for their families.

In an article entitled 'Historical Notes on the Church House at Lustleigh', the building is described as the 'Parish Workhouse' and it seems clear that the present building stands on the 1753 site, that it was used as a house for the poor of the parish, and that the owners were the churchwardens who received rent from the overseers (and paid for repairs of the building). The churchwardens are identifiable as Feoffees of the parish by payment of a 'quit rent', which meant that they held land for property as 'free tenants'.

The original building had a living room and wash-house on the ground floor and rooms over with rough stone walls and a thatched roof and outside steps. In a terrier (inventory) of the church property of 1613, there is mention of a cottage 20' x 17' and a garden 33' x 12' in the parish. Little is known after this until much later, when towards the end of the 19th century things changed. The rector, the Revd Frederic Ensor, died on Christmas Day 1887 and was succeeded by his son-in-law, the Revd Prebendary Henry Tudor, who straightaway set about instituting changes. He decided to refurbish Church House as a parish room which was to be a memorial to his predecessor. The Charity Commissioners consented to this project and the empty Church House was considerably altered. 'A room 34' x 16' with a gallery at one end' was to be made available 'for parochial meetings and reading room or soup kitchen if desired.' The building was to be renamed 'The Ensor Memorial Room' to be used for various social and charitable purposes, a reading room, etc.

Some parts of the scheme fell through but the idea of a memorial continued. A brass tablet over the fireplace in the main room records:

Church House.

Above: *A view of Church House from across the churchyard.*

Below: *Children at work in Lustleigh School, Church House.*

Above: *Interior of Church House, now Lustleigh School.*

This ancient Church House was restored AD1888 by parishioners and other friends, in affectionate remembrance of Frederic Ensor, Rector of Lustleigh, from August 1847 to Christmas 1887.

By 1920, the Church House was in dire need of massive repairs. The sum of £217 was raised by voluntary subscription and an extra £500 followed. The Heavitree Brewery generously gave some land and Church House thereafter continued to be used for parochial and ecclesiastical purposes such as Church Army services and missionary meetings as well as for elections, entertainments, concerts, inquests, etc., but principally as a village reading room. In the more recent past it was also used for 'meals on wheels'.

In 1987 the Church House again required much repair and renovation to fit it for its future use as a small private school. This was achieved through a great deal of hard work and in September 1988 the building was leased to Mrs Christine Hands, the first headmistress, who started a pre-preparatory day school for boys and girls. Its logo, a jenny wren, and an attractive uniform add to what is now a very happy and successful little school with an excellent local reputation where the young are given a wonderful start in life. Mrs Hands retired as headmistress in July 1992 and exchanged roles with her assistant teacher Mrs Jane Dennis, who became head in September 1992. Mrs Hands finally retired in July 1998 and Mrs Dennis continues as head with teaching help. The building is still used occasionally for church and social meetings in the evenings and during the school holidays.

To conclude, it seems appropriate to quote from the last paragraph of the Revd Herbert Johnson's pamphlet, 'Some account of the Church House at Lustleigh':

But there stands our somewhat modest building which has, so far as we know, always been called the Church House. Let it always be preserved, honoured and used. And may it always support the 'Church Life' of Lustleigh, in good and large senses of that expression.

Sources
The Church House by Patrick Cowley.
Report and Transactions of The Devonshire Association Vol. XCV, 1963, p.146.
'Some account of the Church House at Lustleigh' by the Revd Herbert Johnson, MA, Cambridge University Press.
Research by the late Dr Mark Hughes.

The Lustleigh branch of the Rechabites outside the Church House (then known as the Reading Room), c.1907. The Rechabites were members of a teetotal society founded in 1835 and named after Rechab (Jeremiah 35:6).

THE OLD VESTRY
by Veronica Hughes

An inscription on the wall to the left of and above the porch of the Old Vestry in Lustleigh churchyard reads as follows:

OLD VESTRY
1825
BUILT BY SUBSCRIPTION
AND ENDOWED WITH LOWTON MEADOW
IN MORETON
FOR SUPPORTING A SCHOOL FOR EVER
BY THE REV. WILLIAM DAVY
CURATE OF THIS PARISH
UPWARDS OF FORTY YEARS

This building in the churchyard was created by the initiative of the Revd William Davy. When he came as curate to Lustleigh in 1785 there was then no vestry in the church and no village school. Davy lived in the rectory – now a private house, the Old Hall on Mapstone Hill – some half a mile distant from the church and he saw the need for a robing room and a place for meetings and Bible study closer to the church. Besides this practical need he had a strong social conscience and felt that as he himself had received a thorough and free education, others should have the same chance. To further his project he bought the freehold of Lowton Meadow in Moretonhampstead for £325 and stipulated that the rent of £9 per annum should be devoted in perpetuity to the school's upkeep, an endowment which in the years to follow could not be maintained.

The building of granite with a slated roof was to be erected in the north-west corner of the consecrated churchyard and thus owned by the church. The rector's access to it was from the churchyard but the children were forbidden to use this door, their entrance being from the road bordering the boundary of the churchyard. The construction of the school and vestry room met with the approval of the parish although one landlord and his tenant opposed the former as quite unnecessary. Fortunately for the subsequent history of Lustleigh he was outvoted.

William Davy also gave £10 towards the scheme provided that the building was paid for by public subscription and this was agreed. He decreed that the purposes of the school should be for the teaching of 'the Principles of the Established Church, the Word of God, the Catechism, the three Rs, knitting and needlework for the girls.' The rector taught Scripture and the teacher or dame the other subjects. She used a stick for the disciplining of her dozen or so pupils! Education was not always free but some of the more wealthy parishioners would pay the fees for any poor but able child.

A church faculty dated 6 May 1825 authorised the appropriation of a parcel of ground in the churchyard for these purposes and the building work went

A collage of the pictures on the wall of the Old Vestry Meeting Room – Parsons of Lustleigh, from 1847 to 1986. Left to right, top row: William Gordon Baillie (1904), Henry Tudor (1888), Kenneth Jackson (1986), Herbert Johnson (1914), Robert Ryder (1927); centre: Norman McGee (1957); bottom row: Edwin Deacon (1969), Frederic Ensor (1847), Rupert Newman (1945), Arthur Lindsay Palmes (1910).

The Old Vestry from across the churchyard, almost in the shadow of the church.

Re-roofing of the Old Vestry in progress, 1987.

ahead. It was basic – the rector's robing room upstairs, the teacher's or dame's bedroom in what is now the Archives Room, also upstairs, and the schoolroom and living room downstairs. Although one source suggests that the schoolroom was upstairs and the robing room downstairs there is no evidence to support this unlikely arrangement. Water would have been fetched from the village pump; oil lamps and candles used for lighting. No mention is made of a 'privy'! When the school was not in use, it was used for parochial matters – meetings, Bible study and as a reading room. Over many years building repairs, renovations and improvements were made, particularly in 1892.

In 1985 Helen Wood had the idea that the project most needed in Lustleigh at that time was the restoration of the Old Vestry. Her husband, Robert, a retired architect, generously gave his services free as architectural expertise was necessary and he had the enthusiastic support of the then churchwardens, Wallace Kemp and Mark Hughes. It took two years to raise the £15000 needed for the work but Lustleigh residents and visitors came up trumps. The Dartmoor National Park donated Delabole slates for the listed building and many parishioners gave £1 each to have a slate inscribed with his or her name in chalk. This raised £2000 and was an enjoyable and worthwhile team effort for a good cause. A Christow builder, Clarke, did the work which involved removing the entire roof, much rebuilding of the structure, the installation of a kitchen and lavatory, along with much refurbishing of the three main rooms. Bobby and Helen Wood's personal account of this enterprise is shown on page 55.

The state elementary or board school, now privately owned and known as the 'Old School House', was opened in 1876 after the Vestry School closed in the same year, but one must never forget that the old school had served its purpose well for many years and must have educated a large number of children who otherwise would never have had any teaching at all.

In what was originally the schoolroom, but is now used as a meeting room and waiting room, there hang the portraits (some call it the Rogues' Gallery) of Lustleigh's rectors from as far back as 1847. The Reverend William Davy, who was only a curate and not a rector, was nonetheless probably the most important and influential parson of them all. His portrait – as founder of both the Village School and the Vestry building – hangs in pride of place over the mantelpiece.

After the closure of the Church School in 1876, the rent from Lowton Meadow, previously used to support the school, was diverted into three charities for the children. The principal charity was to support

The Old Vestry at the time of writing with Lustleigh Dairy in the background to the left.

the other two and the first was to provide prizes to resident Lustleigh children for 12 months' attendance, a teacher's certificate for good conduct, regular attendance and proficiency, and 15 shillings which would be placed into a child's savings bank account. The second charity was used to reward meritorious members of the Sunday School. In the final years of the last century it became apparent that the original purposes of these charities were no longer being fulfilled and in August 1999 the name and objectives were changed for valid reasons, the re-named charity being called 'The Reverend William Davy's Millennium Bursary Trust'.

The Old Vestry still has its uses today and the rents are used for its upkeep. It is used as a doctor's surgery upstairs twice a week, a waiting room downstairs, and as a space for coffee mornings and sometimes after church services, PCC, Parish Council and British Legion meetings, craft classes, Living Word Library, Church celebrations, polling station,

etc. The Archives Room upstairs – sponsored by the Lustleigh Society and open on Mondays from 10a.m. to 12 noon – houses many important parish documents, including the 1837 Tithe Map, pictures, photographs, newspaper cuttings, *Parish Magazines* dating back to 1888 and much more. It is a mine of information and well worth a visit. It has had a very knowledgeable archivist and is lovingly cared for by a dedicated team from the Lustleigh Society.

Just outside the Old Vestry there are two teak seats; one given by a late parishioner and the other a memorial seat. They are mentioned because, only a few years ago, they replaced two very ancient but rotten oak benches which may once have been church pews.

It is sad to record that the school for which William Davy worked so hard is no more, but the building today is well cared for, loved and used, which is surely as he would have wished.

Right: *Naming the Delabole tiles at £1 each.*

Below: *Tree planting at Criddaford to inaugurate the Old Vestry Restoration Appeal, 1 November 1986. Bobby Wood watches the rector, the Revd Kenneth Jackson, plant a commemorative tree, under the watchful eye of Mrs Anne Jackson.*

The Old Vestry Restoration
by Bobby and Helen Wood

Robert Wood who, with his wife Helen, masterminded the restoration of the Old Vestry in 1985, here tells in his own words the story of how they inspired the village to support the project:

After I retired from architectural practice in July 1985, my wife Helen enquired from the two Misses Raikes if there was a church project that we could help with, to which it was suggested: 'The Old Vestry needs repairing.' The Revd Kenneth E. Jackson was less encouraging with the word 'repair' and suggested that it was 'too expensive to repair, and would probably have to be demolished.'

On examination we found the roof in a very poor condition, with the majority of timbers rotten, and the external walls pushed out at the top and fractured. In other words 'a complete mess'! It was well worth saving – and here was a really worthwhile project – to raise the money and restore the Old Vestry. Wallace Kemp the churchwarden said: 'Get on with it!'

We carried out a survey, drew up plans and submitted a building regulation application to the Council, which included calculations for a new reinforced concrete ring beam to tie in the top of all external walls, then a metal tie bar to stop the walls from spreading, then a complete new roof. We decided to include a little cloakroom and kitchen, sadly lacking in school days. We put our proposals to the church and the village, who were delighted, but a little apprehensive when told of the approximate cost at £15000! It took 12 months for Helen to organise the fund-raising sufficiently to let everyone see the project was serious and up and running! Appeals were sent to all local businesses and many in addition to the architectural world in London. When the fund reached over £10000 and promises of materials and roof slates had been received from Dartmoor National Park we decided that it was time to go to tender. A local firm eventually won the contract to build with a contract figure approaching our budget forecast. It was now all hands to the wheel and how enthusiastic the whole village became. At that time we were landscaping our paddock at Criddaford and Helen had the idea of 'adopt a tree'. We purchased 350 trees and shrubs and planted them in the garden. People were invited to pay one pound, write their name on a label and then tie it to the tree allocated by number. On the first day of November 1986 people streamed into the garden at Criddaford to hear the rector bless the project and assist his wife Anne to plant and name

the first tree. From then on it all went like clockwork, with the 'helpers' showing people around and directing them skilfully to their tree. We had coffee and cakes afterwards and were able to announce a huge total of £735 towards the Old Vestry Repair Fund. The Western Morning News *and the* Herald Express *gave the project publicity and congratulated Lustleigh for their efforts to save their Old Vestry!*

It was not time to rest on our laurels, more money had to be found and it was decided to 'sell' each slate on the roof for £1. People were invited to have their name written on a slate before it was nailed on to the roof. (The Dartmoor National Park had kindly donated all the slates for the roof.) We all took it in turns to sit at a table on the church steps and 'extort' the money from everyone, including any visitor who came to The Primrose Café, The Dairy or The Post Office. Having collected all the money, it was then over to Veronica Hughes and Moira Edmunds to organise writing all the names on the slates – but it was all done and the slates fixed. The restoration work continued. I visited the site every day and the contractors were very good and carried out every detail with expertise. The time came when the contract was complete and the Revd Jackson was handed the key and proclaimed the job 'well and truly complete'. Lustleigh now has a super little building, which houses both the doctor and a room for the Lustleigh Society's archives on the first floor with a parish room complete with kitchen and cloakroom on the ground floor.

The Old Vestry Repair Fund
LUSTLEIGH PARISH CHURCH

Thank You for your Contribution

TREE PLANTING & COFFEE

1st November, 1986.   *10.30 am*

CRIDDAFORD   No. 36.

LUSTLEIGH BAPTIST CHURCH
by Barbara Cutts and Jean Green

For 148 years the little chapel building has stood on the hill overlooking the village. How did it come to be built there? Why was it deemed to be necessary? Some light is shed on the matter in an entry in the 'Diocese of Exeter 1821: Bishop Carey's replies to queries before visitation', produced as *Vol.11 Devon* (1960) by the Devon and Cornwall Record Society, which reads:

The question asked was: "Have you any Papists or Dissenters? If the latter of what kind of denomination? What teachers of each are there resident in your Parish, or occasionally visiting it? Are they licensed? What places have they of Public meeting, licensed, or others?" The reply of John Mudge, Rector of Lustleigh, on 12th May, 1821 was as follows: "No Papists, but many Dissenters they cannot tell themselves of what kind or denomination. No teacher resident in the Parish – the person occasionally visiting it professeth himself a Baptist, licensed. The place of meeting is the Tailors House which is licensed."

The Exeter Record Office lists two meeting-house licences as follows:

25th September, 1809 Ho in poss of Thos Crediford jnr. Application by [1] Wm Wilkins. Minister [2] Thos. Neck [3] Jasper Amery [4] John Amery [5] Wm Bennett [6] Thomas Crediford [7] Thos. Crediford junr [8] Thos. Oliver [9] Abraham Hill [10] Jas. Jackson [11] James Hellier [12] John Bridgman. Inscribed 'Mr. Hatch'.

And a further licence dated 19 December 1835:

GF room in ho at Lower Coombe occ by William Osbourn (sic) lab. Application by [1] Thomas Glanvill of parish of Saint Thomas the Apostle. Devon, Tailor.

Why were these licences required? At the Restoration Nonconformists were regarded as something of a threat to the State, or at least undesirable, and certain penal laws were enacted. However, in 1689 the Toleration Act provided that if a congregation registered its meeting place it was exempt from the penal legislation. The meeting place could be registered at a number of locations including the Bishop's registry and the Quarter Sessions. Things continued thus until 1837 when the Registrar General became responsible as he still is. Registration had real benefits in that it brought the protection of the law against disturbers of worship.

A congregation prepared an application (often several signed) certifying that they had a meeting-

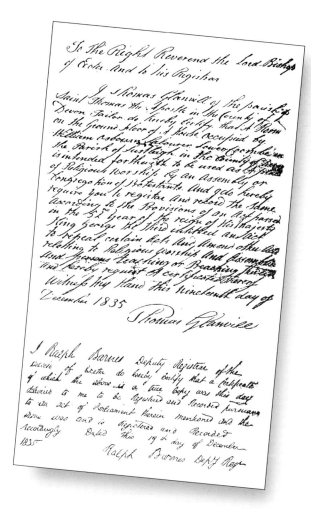

place in use. The authority then issued a 'licence' copying the information on the application certificate. To save travelling into Exeter, etc., many congregations asked a solicitor or minister living in Exeter to make the application. The details were copied into a register and thus the licence was 'registered'. Early certificates were often wholly in manuscript like the 1835 Lustleigh certificate, reproduced above. Although the conveyance relating to the purchase of land on which to build the chapel is dated 20 May 1853, in actual fact this group of dissenting Christians had been meeting together for well over 40 years in private homes in Lustleigh. We have no clue as to who actually built the chapel, possibly it was a do-it-yourself job by the members, but the Devon & Cornwall Baptist Corporation Ltd hold the original conveyance, extracts of which are as follows:

EXTRACTS FROM COPY OF CONVEYANCE, 20th May, 1853 relating to ALL THAT piece of land at Lustleigh, Devon, UPON TRUST for the erection of Ebenezer Chapel, Lustleigh. This indenture made between William Credeford, yeoman of Lustleigh of the one part and

Lustleigh: William Amery and William Amery the Younger both of Ellimore, Yeoman; John Amery and John

Amery the Younger both of Barn, Yeoman; William Amery of Higher Coombe, Yeoman.

Ashburton: John Sparke Amery, Gentleman; James Sparke Evans, Draper; Joseph Aggett, Currier; Nicholas Tarr, Yeoman; Richard Glanville, Tailor.

Moreton-hampstead: Thomas Aggett, Baker; William Sercombe, Grocer.

South Zeal: Edmund Knapman [no occupation given]

Ipplepen: William Lee, Tailor.

WHEREAS the said parties have contracted with the said William Credeford for the purchase of the freehold of the parcel of land hereinafter described for the sum of Five pounds and five shillings.

THAT piece of land containing by admeasurement about 7 poles part of a field or Close of Land called Lower Barley Park, being in the Parish of Lustleigh bounded on two sides by other parts of the said field called Lower Barley Park, on the other side by the public highway leading to the village of Lustleigh aforesaid.

Five of the trustees were common to both Lustleigh and Moreton, some of the trustees of Lustleigh were members of the Moreton Church and some of the trustees in common are buried in the Lustleigh chapel's graveyard. As membership of the Lustleigh Church was of baptised believers it seems almost certain that the trustees would therefore also have been baptised believers and that by 1853 there must have been a strong Baptist influence. The billings in 1857 state 'there is a small Baptist chapel in the village'. No minister was identified. Bovey Tracey Baptist Church minutes record in 1895:

Mr. Tucker reported and Mr. Turner confirmed that the Devon & Cornwall Association committee thought it would be a source of strength spiritually and financially to group together the Moreton, Lustleigh and Bovey Churches under one pastorate if this way of working would be agreeable to the Churches...

The grouping of the Bovey Tracey, Lustleigh and Moreton churches became a fact in 1908 under the ministry of the Revd Way and pastoral care and oversight was then given by the minister of the group, an arrangement which continued until 1945. During 1945 the Moreton church separated from Bovey Tracey and Lustleigh until returning in 1976 when the three congregations became East Dartmoor Baptist Church, then later becoming five congregations with the addition of Chudleigh in 1977 and Christow in 1986.

We must not fail to record that in 1815 a:

Above: *Mr Ernest Wyatt, Manager of the Lustleigh Branch of the Newton Abbot Co-operative Society, with his wife and daughter outside The Dairy.*

... dear brother by the name of Crediford, living at Lustleigh, took an interest in the little Baptist Chapel at Christow, he took such an interest in it, that for five years he walked six miles every Sunday, in each direction, over the roughest of roads, and some of the wildest country to be found in Devon.

A well-known person in Lustleigh in the late 1930s and early 40s was Mr Ernest Wyatt, then Manager of the Lustleigh Branch of the Newton Abbot Co-operative Society, He is seen (*above*) with his wife and daughter outside the shop, now known, of course, as The Dairy.

Mr Wyatt was for many years the Secretary of the Bovey Tracey and Lustleigh Baptist Church. He remembered in the early 1900s, when he was nine or ten years old, occasionally being taken to the chapel at Lustleigh by his father, who conducted worship. He said:

It was afternoon and evening in those days – this meant tea at Miss Allin's or Miss Leaches' home. One recalls the very temperamental slow-combustion heating stove in the chapel which in the course of warming up would belch out clouds of gaseous fumes!

The Revd Leslie Walters flanked by Lionel Treeby on the left and Raymond Tucker on the right, 1950s.

Sunday School when it was held in a tent in the garden of the Lustleigh's Baptist Church.

Sunshine Corner, run by Mrs Tucker.

New windows were installed in 1991, presumably the first since 1853. Our thanks go to Douglas Cooper for his help in the production of this photograph.

Names of faithful folk come to mind such as Miss Annie Allen (who, besides being the Secretary for many years, presided over the sometimes wheezy organ), her brother Richard, Miss Leach and dear old Mrs Wyse; then there was Mrs Meardon, who took over from Miss Allen as the Secretary and organist. The chapel at Lustleigh has a special place in retrospect for me as it was there I preached my first sermon, but the impression that is fixed most firmly in one's memory is the sense of the presence of God being there no matter who was in the pulpit or how few were in the pews, proving conclusively the truth of the promise 'Where two or three gather in my name there am I.'

Some comments by Bernard Treeby, who was organist at the Lustleigh chapel for several years, give an interesting glimpse into life as it was in the mid 1940s. He says:

I have some very warm memories of the people there at that time. Two sisters – Miss Leach and Mrs Keene – cared for the chapel and also the graveyard. They also entertained the preacher and organist to tea after the afternoon service, before we walked out to the main road to catch the bus back. Mrs Meardon (at one time Treasurer, Secretary and chapel caretaker all rolled into one) also took her turn as tea hostess.

Bernard also tells us that sometimes the harmonium had to be taken to someone's house to 'dry out', and recalls: 'On Sundays I often had to take someone along with me to the chapel to lift the notes that had stuck, while I tried to continue playing!'

Sunshine Corner is remembered by a number of people in Lustleigh with obvious pleasure; the photograph taken in the mid 1950s shows the minister, the Revd Leslie Walters who was at Bovey from 1952–58, flanked by Lionel Treeby on the left and Raymond Tucker on the right. Raymond Tucker (who became a very gifted and respected Baptist minister) and Joe Meardon started the meeting when they were in Exeter University, followed by Lionel Treeby and Mrs Freda Tucker, Raymond's mother. The Tuckers were a well-known family of garage owners in Bovey Tracey. Mrs Tucker many years ago said:

I remember the happy years I spent taking 'Sunshine Corner' with the Lustleigh children and how pleased I was when Mrs X...... told me they were always better behaved after they had been to 'Sunshine Corner'!

Len Harvey has told us that liquorice bootlaces were an added incentive to attend!

Over the years children's and youth work has been a very important part of our church life both on Sundays and weekdays. Lack of space has always been a problem even though the pews were replaced by chairs in the 1960s. In that period we had very

fruitful All-Age Worship Services, with three age groups for teaching. Many years later one way of extending the building was to have a tent in the garden for Sunday teaching. By kind permission of the rector of the Parish Church we were allowed to use the Old Vestry for Sunday School when weather no longer allowed the use of the tent. This was an indication of the happy relationship there was, and still is, between the churches in the village. This tent was also used for mid-week clubs and camps.

Opportunities were taken to reach out to the village and beyond. The mid 1980s exhibition of Palestinian models was made by the 'Sunspot' children. Shown in the photograph (*overleaf top right*) are many of those who came to view it including Rosemary Morgan, Ted and Win Robinson and Joan Raikes.

Weekday activities were not confined just to the children and young people; there were also gatherings like 'Welcome Break', the lunchtime get-together. These different kinds of uses for the building were made possible by considerable structural improvements – the installation of a toilet for one. 'We waited 150 years for this' remarked one of our 90-year-old

The entrance as it used to be...

and as it is at the time of writing.

The team of decorators at the chapel, late 1960s.
Mrs Alderton is on the right.

Thelma and Alan Cayley at the right facing camera.

'One-to-one' camp in the Lees' garden in
1989 – meals and group work in the chapel.

Group at the Palestine Exhibition by
the 'Sunspot' children in the mid 1980s.

'Welcome Break' which was held at lunchtime. Included
in the photograph are Jeanne Shipley and George Barron.

A group after Sunday service.

The same group after Sunday lunch.

members, Mrs Alderton of Wood Park, who is pictured in the late 1960s as part of a group who cleaned and decorated the chapel. She was such an inspiration to us all painting the walls using both hands to hold the brush and reaching to the point that she could stretch with her arthritic arms. At one time the only water available was from a tap by the gate but structural improvements through the years have included a useful kitchen area which has recently been much improved once again. The outside has also seen much improvement by the removal of the four steep stone steps and their replacement by a gentler slope more suited to the elderly and disabled.

With the tombstones moved back against the wall, a change deemed necessary for safety, the area was transformed into a pleasant little garden area. We have been known to enjoy Fellowship meals out there, including Easter-morning breakfast, and Songs of Praise have sometimes resounded out over the village.

In 1995 Steve and Janette Brown started the Alpha course with the support of Alan and Thelma Cayley. Alan has, until recently, been the Secretary of East Dartmoor Baptist Church and Thelma is our local Lustleigh Secretary.

So, in conclusion, why do we believe that Lustleigh Baptist Church has a continuing role to play in the life of the village? The answer is because we, as 21st-century Christians, have a precious, hard-won, heritage and a responsibility to stand firm on our belief in freedom of worship, without State control; to hold to the authority of Christ in the Scriptures; and to practise the symbolic act of Believers' baptism by immersion, in accordance with New Testament teaching and as a witness to having come previously to a personal faith in Jesus Christ. 'That which thy fathers have bequeathed unto thee, earn it anew if thou wouldst possess it.'

Note
Acknowledgement is made with gratitude to Roger F.S. Thorne, JP, CEng, MICE, FSA (Hon. Archivist, Plymouth & Exeter District of the Methodist Church) for the information regarding meeting-house licences.

The late Mr Reginald Parker of Boulders who died in 1998 aged 93 and whose father worshipped in the chapel in the early days.

ROMAN CATHOLIC CHAPEL
by Sandro Bullock-Webster

When we arrived in Lustleigh from East Budleigh some 41 years ago it was important to us as a Roman Catholic family to find out where we could go to Mass. In those days new arrivals were often kindly entertained in order to introduce them to other locals. It was at one such gathering that we first met Dolly Walmsley who had built and then maintained her own private chapel beside Pixies Cottage on Mapstone Hill.

I suppose in those days there were between 15 and 20 Catholics who attended Mass there... Dom Rafael Stone, a monk at Buckfast Abbey, would drive over to look after us. Being blind in one eye, he always wore a monocle. He was very keen on music and encouraged us to sing together. Under his tutelage, perhaps, we improved, if only a little. Sadly, he has long since been dead.

Dolly would play the little organ at the back of the church and when Claire, one of her daughters, was there she would provide enormous support to our rather poor vocal efforts. Being a professional singer she was blessed with a very lovely voice.

Each and every Sunday provided a very happy and friendly congregation and I always remember after midnight Mass at Christmas we would all be invited into Pixies Cottage for a glass of punch and hot mince pies.

Dolly Walmsley was not only a very attractive woman, but she also had a personality to match. She was a person who did a lot of public good and had a strong influence for good on others. Profound sadness is the lot of so many people in this life and Dolly was to bear her share when both her granddaughters were killed. Veronica Quantock-Shuldham the elder, was an air hostess and was at that time on the Heathrow-East Africa run. She had been allowed by the company to take her little sister Julia with her for the trip, and on their way back they landed in Addis Ababa. During the take-off the aircraft hit an obstruction that had inadvertently been left on the runway. The pilot braked and swerved, which resulted in a crash, the aircraft burst into flames and the crew and passengers were burnt to death. Both girls were so beautiful and attractive and neither Dolly nor their mother Cicely ever got over this tragedy. Two years before her death in 1984 Dolly moved to live with Cicely near Martock in Somerset.

The sale of Pixies Cottage, with its chapel, heralded the end of a little bit of Lustleigh history.

THE GOSPEL HALL: PLYMOUTH BRETHREN
by Alec N.E. Prowse

Between 1812–20 a group of Christians in New York and also in Great Britain, who were corresponding, felt they needed a simpler, less formal and more spiritual fellowship. The true beginning of the movement started in Dublin, where the first Assembly was formed. This was brought about because some clergy were deliberately denying the authenticity of Holy Scripture and many began to despair of the established Church as the pillar and ground of God's truth. One of these men was the Revd John Nelson Darby, a curate of the Church of Ireland, who proposed to four others a simpler and more Scriptural form of worship in which they began to participate.

He travelled widely across Britain and Europe, preaching in numerous churches; many left their congregations and began to meet in his suggested way. From its inception members have always been fundamentalists, accepting the Holy Bible as the only inspired Word of God, the only infallible and supreme authority.

We believe in Salvation by God's grace alone and not by man's efforts. We believe in the Priesthood of all believers. We believe that the ministry of God's Word is by the enabling of His Holy Spirit and is not an academic qualification. We believe in the return of the Lord Jesus into the air to call all true believers, from whatever denomination, out of this world to be with Him eternally in that place He has gone to prepare. We believe in the punishment in hell to those who reject His offer of mercy and salvation in this life. All these things are Scriptural and the beliefs and teachings of the early Church and they are just as true and relevant to us today. God's Word is eternal.

From 1827 Assemblies began to proliferate across Great Britain and also in other parts of the world. At first, members worshipped in private homes. Places of worship which were called 'Gospel halls' were gradually erected, or purchased, and in time most villages and towns had their own. We believe many souls have been brought into a personal relationship with the Saviour through their witness.

Regarding the Lustleigh Assembly, we do not know exactly when it was formed but we do know that some time in the early 1900s, perhaps earlier, services began to be held in private homes. Then a Mrs L.A. Whiteside made a present of the existing building, at the foot of the Green, available to the Assembly for worship. In her will she left this to Elias White and his son Frank of Brookside, who let it continue as a place of worship. Frank then left it to his son Gordon who allowed the arrangement to continue until 1971 when, for personal reasons, he could no longer be responsible for the place and offered it to the members at a very reasonable price. This was paid by the congregation, who were helped greatly by Mr Birch who gave a large donation and was a member at that time. Appointed trustees are now responsible for its upkeep, etc.

Each Assembly is independent and is overseen by elders chosen by the members to pastor and manage the material and spiritual affairs. An offering is taken after the service of communion or breaking of bread every Sunday morning and all bills and needs are paid from this. The Lord's work at home and in foreign lands, Christian broadcasting and humanitarian needy causes are also supported.

Chapter 3
INDUSTRY & ACTIVITIES

MINING IN THE LUSTLEIGH AREA
by Nick Walter

Lustleigh lies well to the east of the main Dartmoor tin-producing areas. However, there is evidence that tin was extracted from the Wray and Bovey Valleys, and there is one known tin working in the parish. Much more important in recent times was the existence of several lodes of micaceous haematite in the Wray Valley, which were mined up until the 1950s.

Most of the tin working is likely to have taken place in the 15th and 16th centuries when demand for the metal was high. There is documentary evidence that a tin 'blowing house' existed at Caseleigh, and possibly another near the confluence of the Wray and Bovey (1). Some place-names still provide a clue to a now vanished industry, for example two fields that belonged to the farm of Middle Yeo were called 'The Tinwork' and 'The Tinparke'. Middle Yeo was located on the road from Knowle to Wilford Bridge, and was demolished when the railway line was constructed.

Most of the tin-mining activity would have been 'streaming' along the river systems, digging out the tin-rich gravel and crushing, refining and smelting in the local blowing houses. Unlike the open moors, none of the typical banks of spoil are now evident, probably having been destroyed by later farming activity on the fertile valley bottoms. Some underground working may have taken place near Peck Farm, where Peck Pits was recorded in 1822 as a long-disused tin mine. Mining here would probably have been restricted to a series of shallow pit workings in the very wet land between Peck and Sanduck.

In more recent times the local 'shiny ore' mines provided welcome work for local men. A miner's pay was generally higher than a farm labourer's,

Mining Engineer Alexander Livingstone and family at Shaptor Rock around 1890. He had moved to Lustleigh from Scotland to work in the local mines. In 1896 he was in charge of Plumley Mine. He died in 1896 'after a long illness'; pneumonia and 'miner's lung' were occupational hazards for miners at that time.

although the risks were also greater. Mrs Lilian Jones remembered:

There were some iron mines in the parish, and once a Mr Druett got killed, and I well remember his mates carrying his body home on a wooden stretcher covered by a sheet.

George Druett of Brookfield was buried on 11 June 1910.

A History of Kelly Mine

Kelly Mine lies on the eastern edge of the parish of Lustleigh and has been an integral part of village life for 200 years. The mine is currently leased by the landowner – Mrs Molly Amery of Kelly Farm – to the Kelly Mine Preservation Society who have been restoring the site since 1984. The material mined at Kelly is a form of iron oxide, scientifically known as micaceous haematite, but always known locally as 'shiny ore'. The local area contains many small veins of this ore in the granite, the veins being almost vertical and varying in width from an inch to several feet. It is thought the iron formed due to the circulation of superheated water in the cooling granite. This would have contained minerals in solution and forced its way through cracks in the rock, altering the granite and depositing various minerals as it cooled. The 'shiny ore' deposits between Bovey Tracey and Moretonhampstead were the only commercially viable deposits found in Great Britain.

Micaceous haematite consists of tiny flakes of iron oxide, which when dry have a grey metallic sparkle. The best ore is relatively soft but heavy, and the ore veins usually run eastwards. The flaky nature of the ore gives it several useful properties. Its first known use was in the late-18th century, when used as a blotting powder, being sprinkled over wet ink on documents to absorb the surplus liquid. Fine beach sand and powdered cuttlefish were also used, but the shiny ore seems to have been highly valued. Close scrutiny of the signatures of contemporary papers can sometimes reveal the tiny flakes of silvery ore in the dried ink. With the introduction of better quality paper and ink the demand for blotting powder disappeared. By that time other uses had been found for the ore, believed to include mixing with graphite, an unspecified use in chemical works, and in specialist use in iron and steel manufacture (possibly as a catalyst or release agent).

The bright appearance of the ore resulted in its use in the local pottery industry as a part of the glaze. Poorer quality ore was also used as an alternative to graphite grease. In 1876 Ephraim Yeo of Newton Abbot patented a mixture of hemp yarn, grease and shiny ore for use as a packing agent in steam engines. Around 1890 there was a surge in demand for the ore because it was found to be ideal as a base for

Bill Crocker and Francis Heath at the Slade workings in 1951. Ore extracted here was taken to Kelly Mine for sorting and crushing before trucking to Pepperdon Mine for finishing off and packing. Des Waldron, the Lustleigh coal merchant, was contracted to transport ore between the two sites.

Blasting at Slade in 1951 resulted in a major collapse into previously undiscovered older mineworkings. In Francis Heath's words 'You could look right down; the 'old men' had been there before us.' Here Bill Crocker and Francis Heath are pictured in the hole. This collapse and the failure to find new lodes resulted in the closing down of all operations at Slade, Pepperdon and Kelly mines.

corrosion-resistant paint. The flakes of iron oxide form an overlapping and waterproof layer on iron and steel. This was used in warship grey paint, as well as on bridges and locomotives, and it was regarded as the best protection in extreme conditions. This type of paint is still used but the flakes are now produced artificially, mainly because no commercially viable ore deposits remain.

The first record of Kelly Mine occurs in 1797, when Kelly Farm was sold by John Pinsent to George Wills. John leased back for 21 years 'a certain mine of black lead or some other substance' at South Kelly. In 1822 Daniel Lysons wrote the following:

In the parishes of Hennock and Lustleigh, there is found in the granite a species of micaceous or peculiar iron-ore, known by the name of Devonshire Sand. A few tons of this article were sent some years ago from Exeter to London where it was used for writing sand, and various other purposes, it was sold at from three to eight guineas a ton.

Small-scale production seems to have continued for some years, as Mr Wills of Kelly was advertising shiny ore for sale in 1841. The first official record of the mine appears in Government mining records for 1877, when the mine was leased by the Kelly Iron Company, with well-known local mining engineer William Henry Hosking directing operations. For the next ten years or so production varied from 20 to 30 tons a year, with two or three workers employed. The ore at this time is quoted as having sold for about £3 a ton.

In 1892 mining ceased, and the mine was advertised to let, 'being equipped with waterwheel and stamps for ore dressing'. It seems to have remained closed until 1900, when the Scottish Silvoid Company took over. They appear to have invested heavily in new buildings and equipment, probably sinking the shaft still visible today. The workforce increased to between six and eight workers and production during the first years of the 20th century averaged 150 tons a year. Samuel Hill of Lustleigh was the mine captain at the beginning of the century.

Scottish Silvoid worked the mine until 1917, when the Ferrubron Company took over the lease. This company then owned Great Rock Mine at Hennock and had previously operated several local shiny ore mines, including Shaptor, Hawkmoor and Plumley. The Ferrubron Company stopped work at Kelly around 1944, due to lack of ore reserves and a shortage of labour owing to the war. This was the last underground activity at the mine, though the processing machinery was used from 1948 to 1951 by the company running Pepperdon Mine.

The last activity at Kelly Mine was in the early 1950s when Nicols & New, the firm now operating Pepperdon Mine, used the Kelly machinery to process ore obtained from an underground working between Kelly and Slade Cross. However, blasting in 1951 caused a major collapse into undetected earlier workings. Francis Heath, one of the miners, recalled those last days when desperate attempts were made to find new ore deposits:

Totters said, 'There's beautiful lode over there.' We got a horse and cart from Kelly Farm and dug out the lode in the field. We took out ten bags of good ore and that's all there was. Mr Nicols said to Totters 'You been pulling the wool over my eyes.'

The failure to find new lodes and the collapse of the Slade workings resulted in the closing down of all operations at Slade, Pepperdon and Kelly mines.

At Kelly the buildings were locked and left undisturbed for many years, still containing all the mining machinery. Thus Kelly Mine retained a unique collection of mining equipment, which despite the attentions of souvenir hunters was still virtually complete when restoration work started in 1984. Working at Kelly in the final years were Sid Beard, Harry Moore, Francis Heath, Bill Crocker and Arthur 'Totter' Horrell. Bob Gilbertson of Lustleigh worked at Pepperdon Mine at the same time. The local connection with mining did not end then, as several Lustleigh people worked at the nearby Great Rock Mine until that closed in 1969. These included Dave Wills, Tony Bunclark and Tony Haydon-Baillie.

Typically around half the mine workforce would work underground, extracting the soft ore with picks, bars and shovels. The surrounding granite would then be drilled or blasted to access the next section of the lode. Much of the waste rock was stacked in worked-out sections of the mine, often placed on timbers wedged above the access passages. The miners used candles for lighting until the 1930s when carbide lamps were introduced. Surface workers would be employed in sorting and washing the ore, operating the machinery, and drying and packing ore. From Kelly the dry ore was packed in barrels and taken to Lustleigh Station by cart. When the photograph on page 66 was taken the typical miner's pay would have been just over £1 a week, with surface workers earning slightly less. Jack Joint, who worked at Kelly in 1927, remembered, 'It was not a bad job. It was paying more than anywhere else. But they were hard times and you had to do a day's work.'

Restoration work at Kelly Mine started in 1984 after the formation of a preservation society and the negotiation of a lease with the landowners. Since then the buildings and machinery have been carefully restored, original features being retained wherever possible. Society members have also carried out research into local mining history and much useful information has been obtained from local people. Several ex-miners have been traced and interviewed, and their memories have been invaluable in the

Tony Bunclark at the winding shaft,
Great Rock Mine, 1962.

Tony Haydon-Baillie with a compressed-air
rock drill at Great Rock Mine in 1962.

The above photograph shows the Kelly Mine workforce of 1907 standing in front of the shaft which was then being used to mine the shiny ore. This photograph was given to the Lustleigh Society by Mrs Lilian Jones. Her father John David Johns is the miner on the far right. He was probably mine foreman at the time, and living at Brookfield, as many of the miners did. John Johns died in 1913 of 'miner's lung'. Thanks to Mr Bill Squires and Dr Tom Greeves most of the miners pictured have been identified. From left to right they are Bill Squires, Jabus Hill, Ernest Squires, Walter Squires, ?, Lewin Hill and John Johns. The Squires and Hill families were both from Lustleigh. The shaft is situated behind Ernest and Walter Squires, who are posing with one of the tipping and rotating trams unique to these mines. The machinery behind Jabus Hill is thought to be a pump, probably powered by the 'flat rods' visible above Bill Squires. Most of the miners are wearing 'Yorks', straps around their trousers just below the knee. These kept the trouser bottoms clear of the worst mud and minimised wear on the cloth when kneeling.

reconstruction work. The following extracts give a graphic picture of a vanished lifestyle.

Cliff Wills was 14 when he started work at Kelly Mine:

I started work on May Day 1938. I remember the day because they always had a maypole in Lustleigh village in those days and I could hear the music coming across the fields. When I was there, I worked with Bill Hines, Claude Hellier and another bloke from Lustleigh called Walt Lethbridge. The foreman was Jimmy Stancombe. My first job each morning was to walk up into the woods and turn on the water. I used to put down rabbit snares on the way up in the morning and collect the rabbits in the evening when the water had to be turned off. Normally we used the turbine but had to use the engine in the summer to conserve the water for washing the 'shiny ore'. All the machinery was driven by belts and when I was there a law came in that all the belting had to have guards. It was a tedious old job screening all the belts and the engine and I had the job of creosoting the wood.

You had to keep a steady feed into the stamps and make sure the heads were evenly loaded. You could make the stamps play a tune if they weren't. Jimmy Stancombe, over in the hut, could hear when the stamps needed feeding and he would call out. We learned all the tricks about ore-dressing from Jimmy.

I often had to cycle over to Lustleigh, to Osborne's baker's shop, to buy baccy and pasties for the men but I usually brought a dish of grub – a roast dinner from the day before – and heated it up on the stove in the hut. I often got sent up into the woods at Kelly to cut timber for the mine. We used timber a lot, usually larch and Douglas fir. Miners liked these because the wood 'talked' when the ground squeezed it and gave them a good warning. At Kelly there was only one adit in use in my time, down by the road at the bottom of the incline. Everything had to be hauled up, there was no room down by the road for the waste.

Most days when there was ore I had the job of washing it. The gravel and sand settled out and I had to keep shovelling it back up until all the colour had gone. When it had been dried the ore was very runny, you couldn't pick it up with your hands as it would run through your fingers. The full barrels were taken over to Lustleigh Station by the Great Rock lorry. Kelly had a truck of coal over at Lustleigh Station. It was brought over to the mine in a horse and cart by Farmer Amery down at Kelly Farm. The miners used to help out with the harvest in the afternoon, they did it for the cider. This was made in the cider press down at the farm.

I went on the annual outing when I was at Kelly, we all went at the end of August. I am pretty sure we went up to Wells as I remember seeing the great clock in the cathedral.

The ore ran into the cement settling tanks. They would hold about 10 tons and took about four or five months to fill. The tanks were 'speared' every day to

help with the settling. Little square shovels were used for digging out the ore. Three shovelfulls were enough for a barrow load, it was so heavy.

Jack Joint worked at Kelly Mine from 1927 to 1928:

I was at Kelly for two years. I know that because there were two annual outings when I was there, it was always on the first Saturday in August. There were nine men working at Kelly in those days. Charlie Parker – he was on trams. Captain Stancome – mine captain. Walter Lethbridge – he used to work down in the drying shed. Fred Lethbridge – the mine blacksmith. Bill Hines – miner. A man called Down – I think he lived up the Teign Valley. Hellier – miner, he was a tall bloke, couldn't read or write, rather odd even in those days. Arthur (Totter) Horrell – miner. Myself – ore-washing.

I was 16 when I first worked here. There were no trees, it was all open. I had a little washing place, it had a galvanised roof over it. There used to be a little stream running down the side from which we got the water. Used to get our clothes all wet, we dried them in the grub-hut overnight.

Fred Lethbridge was the blacksmith. He used to work at the anvil sharpening the drills and picks. The picks were sharp one end and flat at the other. He would get them bright bluey-red in the forge and hammer them into shape. He dipped them into water to harden them.

There used to be a tramway up above the grub-hut. They tipped the ore into the wash and also tipped it into the shed for the stamping machine. The stamps had three heads – made an awful racket. They were worked by water power. There would be one man in there shovelling the ore under the stamps. We used to have our meals in the grub-hut. The stove used to be in the middle of the floor – you can see where it used to be, the hole is still in the ceiling. There was no sink or hot water then, we just used the stream for washing.

The miners didn't wear helmets. A candle was stuck anywhere they were working with a lump of clay. There were two sets of rails, one to Bottom Level and one to Middle Level. They used metal trams, there were no wooden trams in my day. You had to go along to Middle Level to fill your tram. I had to keep my eyes skinned for bits of gold. It was stuff call mundick, like gold but paler, we had to throw this away. I managed to get a motorbike when working at the mine. I got the going rate for the job – mining was the best paid job around. It was a nice job except when the weather was bad, and then we had some shelter. There were some lovely views in those days before the trees all grew up.

These reminiscences and excavations on site have been vital in the restoration of Kelly Mine. The Preservation Society would like to thank all the local people and ex-miners for their assistance. Special thanks are due to the Amery family and Dartmoor National Park Authority.

ASH HOUSES IN & AROUND LUSTLEIGH

by Jeff Cushman

This short account of Dartmoor ash houses is based on a talk, given to the Lustleigh Society in October 1992, by Roger Perry – one-time Lustleigh resident – who had made a special and detailed study of these curious structures.

Ash houses, as their name implies, were used as a safe repository for hot wood ash from domestic fires to avoid sparks from embers catching light to thatched roofs. They were also a place where the ash could be kept dry before being used to supply potash to be used on arable fields.

Few ash houses occur outside south-east Dartmoor and of the 38 known to the National Park Authority, 24 of which are listed, some 85 per cent are in Lustleigh, Manaton, North Bovey, Chagford and Moretonhampstead parishes. They are thus a very local phenomenon a fact for which no one has suggested a reason. Indeed, because of their local nature, there is very little literature about them. They appear not to be mentioned at all in *Crossing's Guide* and although Worth speaks of them, he claims that the ash was emptied at night which is at variance both with common sense and the recollections of people today who have heard their parents or grand-parents talk of their use.

All Dartmoor ash houses are built of granite rubble with roughly dressed stones used for lintels and quoins. Most are circular with a conical roof of corbelled stones which was probably covered with turf to preserve the lime mortar between them and keep the whole waterproof. They usually had a rectangular hatch near the top of the wall through which the ashes were tipped down a slight slope through the thickness of the wall which could be as much as two feet. Opposite the hatch there was

customarily a doorway from which a cart could be loaded when the ash, mixed with manure, was to be spread on the land. Both the hatch and the doorway would have had metal doors. In half a dozen cases the hatch doors have survived but only at Bowden in North Bovey is the fireproof main doorway still present.

In general ash houses were sited some 10–40 paces from the house to balance safety from fire with convenience of use; the hatch would have faced towards the house and opposite would be the door where a cart could be drawn up for loading. The diameter of the circular ash houses was to some extent limited by the roof construction and averaged about six feet internally. Height varied and the taller ones often had outside steps to enable the housewife to reach the hatch.

A number of rectangular ash houses also exist. Some of these have roofs made of granite slabs laid crosswise and cut by the 'feather and tare' technique which only came in at the start of the 19th century. One such is at Waye Farm. There are several variants of the basic design. Some, for example, are built into hedge banks and the one at Morecombe Farm, Moretonhampstead, has two hatches, one above the other instead of the more usual doorway opposite. Sometimes it is hard to be sure, in cases where their original use has been changed, whether the buildings have ever been used as an ash house or actually started life as a kennel or a goose house.

Probably no ash houses are more than 300 years old and a number of rectangular ones seemingly date from the 19th century. Their use died out as the century progressed bringing with it rail and improved road transport which in turn brought coal for domestic fires and artificial fertilisers for the land. Few, if any, of today's farmers remember them being used but some people recall being told about them by their older relatives.

Ash house at Bullaton of a simple structure. The ashes were loaded and removed through a single door.

A simple Lustleigh ash house with typical corbelled stone roof but only a single door.

Top left: *The roof of the square ash house at Waye Farm is composed of stone rubble supported by cleft granite posts. The doorway can be seen on the lower left with the smaller, higher entrance hatchway on the adjoining wall.*

Top right: *Well preserved listed ash house at Lower Hisley retains a traditional corbelled stone roof.*

Left: *Typical small round ash house at Lussacombe with replacement thatched roof.*

Above: *The ash house at Sanduck, sited on the far side of the road, has a small square hatchway on the north side opposite the doorway, which is now blocked.*

Dartmoor National Park has restored some of the existing ash houses whereas others have been converted to such new uses as dog kennels, garden stores, and even a goat house at Narrowmore. At Drewsteignton one has been part glazed and thatched and turned into a summer-house. Others sadly have been neglected and fallen into disrepair; the one at Foxworthy (on the north-west margin of Lustleigh) has only the foundations left. Another, in Moretonhampstead, whose new owner did not realise its significance, was recently demolished.

What is so puzzling about ash houses is their very local occurrence. Why should they be concentrated in south-east Dartmoor? Granite is perhaps the key; easily and always available, it was and is cheap, durable and fireproof. On the west side of Dartmoor, while there was plenty of granite, there was more employment of Cornish and other slate for the roofing of farm buildings in place of the characteristic Devon thatch; moreover the rainfall is much higher in the west and for these reasons there was less call for fire precautions. Additionally the then extensive arable farming on the east side of the moor undoubtedly benefited from the extra potash so conveniently stored and accessible for spreading on the land.

FARMING THROUGH THE CENTURIES

by Ann Jones

Like so many small rural villages Lustleigh was originally carved out of the woods and forests which covered the landscape. For many centuries the principal work was to be found on one of the many farms around the village. Being a hilly area the farms tended to be small and though much of the land could be ploughed, there were also some fields down to grass. In those days farmers had to be self-sufficient and their farms would have had something of everything – cattle, pigs, chickens, sheep and geese, and some fields of wheat, barley and oats as well. Potatoes, peas and leeks or onions would also be grown, and the wives all had their own patches of herbs. All farmers had their own orchards growing the apples needed for eating and especially cider making, the popular local drink considered essential in the farming community.

This type of farming went on for many hundreds of years with the small fields surrounded by banks, often with hedges on top, or plain hedges which would be cut and laid every ten or fifteen years to re-new and strengthen them. These hedges would have a mixture of plants in them though the most important one was usually hazel which grows well around here. Not only was it considered a desirable hedge plant but it also provided edible nuts in the autumn, much enjoyed by people and animals alike. Other plants used were hawthorn, blackthorn, holly, oak, ash, willow and alder. Wild rose, bramble, sloe, wild cherry and spindle could also be found in the hedges. On some farms stone walls were also used between the fields.

For centuries the only form of transport was the horse, whether ridden or used as pack animals. With the pack saddles 'crock' or 'crooks' were used – long, shaped pieces of wood of different sizes depending on the job in hand. When carrying stone, gravel, lime or manure, wicker baskets which opened at the bottom were the solution. They were large enough to hold about 1cwt each or just over 50kg. Wheeled horse carts or wails were used at some of the more affluent and flatter farms around 1740 as shown by the Wyndham Survey of the Manor of Lustleigh in 1742 which includes a reference to a 'wain house' at South Harton. The smaller, steeper farms however generally did not use wheeled carts for another 100 years or so. All the surplus from the farms would be taken to a local market such as Moretonhampstead or Bovey Tracey, and rather later to Newton Abbot, the only one to have survived to the present day.

As the farms were rather small there were quite a number of them in the parish, over 20 or so in all, ranging from around 20 acres to about 150 acres. On the western side of the parish is the Cleave *(see page 26)*, a large tract of rough land on which certain farms had grazing and other rights. Many changes have come about since the mid-20th century and most of the farms are now all grass, usually grazed by sheep and cattle. A majority of the old farms are now private houses and the actual number of farmers has plummeted to about three. There are still some very old farmhouses in Lustleigh such as Waye, Higher Hisley, Lower Coombe and Foxworthy, though several were re-built after being burnt down when their thatched roofs caught fire, many during the last 200 years.

In the fields above Knowle Road;
a two-horse plough for potato planting.

70

A group of parishioners pauses for refreshment during the beating of the bounds in 1924.

Harvesting in times past. A group at Kelly Farm pause for a rest in the 1930s.

The motive force for all farming, 1904. Mr Payne, the farrier, outside his forge in the centre of Lustleigh village.

Left: *Haymaking in the 1920s.* Left to right: *Mrs Aggett, Margaret Amery, Ivy Aggett, Betty Chilcott, Fred Amery (farmer), Joe Amery, Perce Dyer, Fred Aggett.*

Below left & right: *Before the use of gates and hinges fields were enclosed by posts and rails. Here are two posts at Lower Hisley; originally the slots faced each other across the opening; one end of a rail was pushed into a slot in the post and the other end was then slid to be dropped into the L-shaped slot in the second post.*

Lustleigh Apple Day

Ray Williams, the expert, formerly with the Long Ashton Research Station, helps to identify varieties.

Villagers watch him work high in a tree.

Hugh Gould (hand on chin) looks up to watch Ray Williams at work.

Lustleigh Apple Day

Barry Sessions prepares to plant a new tree.

Les Reid unloads his basket of apples in the trailer bound for the cider press.

Liam Carnell uses a long stick as an unorthodox picking aid.

Lustleigh Apple Day

Old trees are grubbed and new varieties planted.

New varieties growing happily.

Tea and demonstration as part of Apple Day, 1992.

Lustleigh Apple Day

AN ... ...APPLE A DAY

Eight-year-old Emma Reid tries one of the 100 varieties of apples on show at Lustleigh from the Devonshire Apple Sanctuary.

LUSTLEIGH'S first Apple Day was a resounding success on Saturday, with visitors coming to the village from far and wide for a range of separate events.

Mr Edward O'Donnell, of the Devonshire Apple Sanctuary, talked on the history of the apple and 100 different varieties were on show. Apple expert Mr Ray Williams gave a talk and demonstration on pruning

and identified various varieties on request.

There was a tour of the Orchard, several exhibitions, including a photo record of former Lustleigh May Queens, and entertainment from the local choir and drama group.

All proceeds will go to the Lustleigh Orchard and Village Hall Fund.

Left: *Apple stalls in the Village Hall; experts were on hand to identify different varieties.*

Above: *'An apple a day keeps the doctor away.' Eight-year-old Emma Reid enjoys an apple from the Town Orchard.*

Below: *The case for conserving traditional mixed orchards is a compelling part of the demonstration.*

THE RAILWAY

by Jan Rowe

'Before the railway brought outsiders in, there was hardly anybody in the place who did not own land or rent it or work on it, and nobody at all who did not talk of it.' (Cecil Torr, *Small Talk at Wreyland, Vol. II*)

The 1851 census showed Lustleigh as an exclusively rural and farming village. The population consisted predominantly of farmers, farm labourers and the craftsmen needed to support the farms and the village way of life. Of the 39 households in the village the occupations at that time were:

Landed proprietor	1
Farmers	8
Farm labourers	16
Carpenters	4
Shopkeeper	1
Blacksmith	1
Wheelwright	1
Cordwainer	1
Tailors	2
Millers	2
Others	2

By this time, however, the railways were changing the whole country and Lustleigh was to change too. The railway system was developing fast, with the Main Line linking Bristol, Taunton and Exeter opening in 1844. Within the next few months work had begun on the South Devon Railway between Exeter, Teignmouth, Totnes and Plymouth. This line began operating in 1849. Branch lines followed on very quickly and in the late 1850s a group of prominent landowners decided that a company should be formed to construct a line from Moretonhampstead to the South Devon Main Line at Newton Abbot. In September 1861 the promoters met at the Globe Hotel in Exeter to form a committee to negotiate with landowners and to set up the Moretonhampstead and South Devon Railway Company.

On 7 July 1862 the Bill for making a railway from Newton Abbot to Moretonhampstead received the Royal Assent. Among the six Directors of the new company was Thomas Wills of East Wrey, Lustleigh. Work began in 1863. Delays during the winter of 1864–5 were due to bad weather, but by spring 1865 the major earthworks were substantially complete. Work was finished in the early months of 1866, and having passed the Board of Trade inspection, the branch was formally opened on Tuesday 26 June 1866. Opening Day was celebrated as a public holiday with many people turning out to witness the first train on its journey from Newton Abbot to Moretonhampstead.

Cecil Torr's grandfather was initially worried that the new railway, with its 'raw and glaring' cuttings, would spoil the surrounding landscape, but Cecil Torr himself was full of praise for the line's well-proportioned granite viaducts which strode across the Devon countryside with a Roman grandeur. He considered that, had they been transported to Italy and attributed 'to Roman or Etruscan builders', in all likelihood 'artists would have flocked to paint them.'

Train heading towards Newton Abbot, passing the Cleave Hotel.

Lustleigh Station in the early years of the 20th century.

However, the construction of the railway had not been without its problems. Writing in 1864 Cecil Torr's grandfather described the behaviour of the imported navvies:

More than a hundred (navvies) discharged on Monday, and a pretty row there was: drunk altogether, except one couple fought in the meadows for an hour and got badly served, I hear. The same night the villains stole all poor old ***'s fowls. He had them under lock and key, but they broke in and took the whole, young and old... There is not a fowl or egg to be got hereabout.

Writing in 1865 he describes a visit from a drunken navvy the day before – 'about as fine a built tall likely a fellow as you ever saw, and nicknamed the Bulldog'. He asked for meat and drink and was sent empty away. 'I learnt that he worked Saturday and Monday, and received 5s.6d. for the two days, slept in a barn and spent all his earnings at the public house.'

The granite stones with which the bridges were built were cut and dressed from the rocks on Lustleigh Cleave. Horses and carts were used to bring the stones from the Cleave to the building site where they were required. The horses were stabled in one of the barns at Waye, and on one occasion the barn caught fire and was badly burnt. Presumably the horses were rescued in time by the drivers living in the house. There was no fire engine in those days and the blaze had to be fought with buckets of water.

On completion, the broad-gauge line was 12 miles, 28 chains in length, with intermediate stations at Bovey Tracey and Lustleigh, and later at Teigngrace. The initial train service provided a basic pattern of four up and four down workings between Newton Abbot and Moretonhampstead, all being worked by the South Devon Railway. In 1872 the Moretonhampstead and South Devon Railway became fully amalgamated with the South Devon Railway and a few years later, in 1878, was absorbed by the Great Western Railway. Life in the country-side was changing fast. Coal, timber and fertilisers could be delivered more easily and cheaply, the mail arrived promptly, and local crops could reach a wider market. Jack Heal recorded his memories of his working life on the railway in the early years of the 20th century:

When I was on the railway I used to deliver Silcox meal. They used to come in the wagons sometimes and it was cowcake, dairy nuts and fattening nuts. I used to deliver that around to the farms... the farmers used to order it by the Traveller that used to go around and then they used to send it by rail.

In 1892 the old broad-gauge line was converted to narrow gauge. The *Parish Magazine* of June 1892 recorded that:

... a very wonderful work has been carried on, the conversion of the Broad to Narrow Gauge. 5000 men were employed and in some 32 working hours this

great feat was accomplished... On Sunday night at 9pm a Service was held on the railway by Casely Woods, close to the tents, for the sixty men who had worked on this part of the Moreton line... Mr. Richards, of our choir, helped to make the singing of the three hymns hearty, and a very attentive congregation met for the first and probably the last time on the railway by Casely Woods.

After the building of the railway the countryside returned to normal. Eventually the landscape recovered and Cecil Torr commented:

Now that the cuttings and embankments are all overgrown and covered with verdure, one can hardly realise how hideous it looked when they were raw and glaring.

The railway brought Standard Greenwich or 'railway time', and the electric telegraph which was installed at the Lustleigh Post Office on 3 May 1893. The *Parish Magazine* declared that:

The Telegraph at the Post Office has been of great use, especially in times of illness or accident, and even poor people have found it quicker and cheaper to telegraph to the Doctor than to go by train to ask him to come.

Movement around the countryside and to distant places became much easier. In July 1890 the men of the Lustleigh Church Choir and the Ringers elected 'in spite of the very long journey, to join the Newton Choir party and go to Hereford and Malvern'. 'They will pass through the Severn Tunnel, and see an old Cathedral, and a part of England unknown to them', promised the *Magazine*. The first school excursion of children, teachers and parishioners went to Teignmouth by train on Saturday 1 September 1894. The journey from London to Exeter, which in the preceding century had taken four days, by the 1890s took only four and a quarter hours.

Communications were much improved. Letters posted in the morning were delivered in Exeter, Newton Abbot, Plymouth and Torquay on the same day. The station became the most important place in the community. It was the place from where everyone came and went, where news came in from the world outside either by letter, telegraph, newspaper or by word of mouth. Most lines ran 'Best Kept Garden' competitions and Lustleigh's station garden was highly regarded.

However, the anticipated influx of new residents did not happen to any great degree. According to Cecil Torr:

When the railway came, a plan was drawn up showing how the hillsides were to be laid out with winding roads and villas in the accepted Torquay style; and two such villas were built, but happily no further harm was done.

A number of new houses were built in the latter part of the 19th century but there was no great impact on the population. From 1801 to 1901 population figures

Wreyland Path and the railway line, 1907. The railway station can just be seen at the far right.

for Lustleigh show a steady, though small, increase over the decades, from 246 in 1801 to 400 in 1901. The train service, in fact, was never all that convenient from the point of view of local residents who frequently asked for more passenger trains. The *Parish Magazine* in March 1891 contained this report:

It is rumoured that some additional trains are likely to be soon put on the Moreton line, in consequence of many requests to the Directors of the Great Western Railway, and that a train will leave Moreton about 9.20am and that an afternoon train will leave Newton about 3.15pm. Even if this afternoon train was only on Market Days it would be a great convenience to many people, especially to those who have to drive some miles after their railway journey, and an afternoon train would tend, we believe, to promote sobriety and comfort in some homes in this district.

The branch passenger service was so sparse that it did not serve the needs of businessmen or professional people who instead preferred to live in Torquay or other fashionable residential areas.

Tourism, on the other had, did flourish. Lustleigh had been popular with walkers and holiday makers before the advent of the railway, but now the visitors came in even greater numbers. Services for tourists grew rapidly. There were hotels, guest-

houses, apartments and rooms as well as cafés, refreshment rooms and carriages to transport the visitors. There was a holiday coach in the station yard.

By the 1920s the service industry probably employed more people than farming. In 1906 the GWR introduced a motor-bus service between Moretonhampstead and Chagford which encouraged further tourist traffic on the line. Tourist publications were produced, such as Methuen's *Little Guide to Devon* in which Lustleigh was described as a 'beautifully situated village' surrounded by 'much disintegrated granite, with curious weathered granite blocks like huge loaves'. Encouraged by such publications the numbers of tourists increased and the Stationmaster at Lustleigh took to keeping a visitors' book in his waiting-room.

Local business grew and prospered. There was a Post Office and General Stores, two butchers, a baker and a coal merchant. In 1904 a Co-operative Society shop was introduced. Nurseries were able to take advantage of the ease with which perishable goods could be transported. The Easton family were builders and carpenters, and the village still supported the work of two blacksmiths. Rabbit-trapping became a lucrative business. Florence Amer, describing her childhood in Lustleigh, records that, in the early years of the 20th century, her father was a self-employed rabbit-trapper 'sending away by

The last passenger train to Lustleigh, 1959.

rail many thousands of rabbits to the large cities, mostly in the Midlands – Birmingham, Nottingham, Manchester and Leicester.' She continues:

Until some of my brothers were old enough to help in the business my father employed a man... I remember how my mother would smuggle a brace or two of rabbits away out of sight during the packing into hampers for dispatch to the station, to pass on to one or two of our less fortunate friends.

With the increase in businesses and services, and the railway itself, there were more opportunities for employment at a time when farming was in decline. Cecil Torr writes:

When it was a novelty here, our line had great attractions for young men and boys and many of them left their work on the land. I lost sight of one family for 30 years or more, and on inquiry I found their history was this; 'Well, one of 'n went on the line and he became a station-master, 'nother he went on the line and he became a ganger, and t' other, he were runned over by a train; and so, as us may say, they was all connected with the railway.'

Despite the advantages that the railway brought to the rural economy and the fact that local industries and crops had access to wider markets, it could not halt the steady decline in farming. The chief crops of the area were wheat, barley, potatoes and turnips. In the mid-19th century the arable farming in the village was able to support two working mills but by the end of the century there had been a marked change in favour of mixed farming with beef and sheep supplying the market at Newton Abbot.

The period of growth of services in Lustleigh was 1860–1930s. After this there was a steady decline. Larger urban areas, more accessible because of the railway, bus services and the private car, grew at the expense of smaller communities. The smaller tradespeople left due to the competition from larger shops and more choice at competitive prices in the towns. The carriers were finished by 1940 and the blacksmith, the miller and the rabbit-catcher had disappeared.

From the beginning the branch lines had always struggled financially. In the initial enthusiasm to promote the building of a line which was intended to bring prosperity to the local community, the costs of building routes over difficult terrain, of borrowing capital and of paying a huge workforce were largely understated. Often there was no proper assessment of the traffic potential or awareness of the particular social and economic needs of the area. Many local lines found themselves unable to cover the normal running costs as well as keep reserves to meet emergencies and to service loans. This was certainly the problem for the Moretonhampstead branch line.

Most of the passenger income came from the third-class journeys, and though summer tourist traffic was significant, the income from local traffic was not enough to cover routine working expenses. Dividends steadily declined in the last third of the 19th century while costs rose. With the increase in bus services and the use of the private motor car the branch railway could no longer compete, and the line was allowed to run down. In May 1957 the *Mid Devon Advertiser* revealed that the closure of the Moretonhampstead branch railway line was under consideration. Following this, in March 1959, the *Western Morning News* reported that 'the last train came down the Moreton line... to the clamour of detonators and whistle shrieks and 'Auld Lang Syne.' That was the end of the passenger service. Freight services continued for a little longer. After serving the needs of local people for almost a century the railway age for Lustleigh had come to an end.

LUSTLEIGH MILLS
by Jan Rowe

Follow the course of the little stream running from the bridge below the church and you will come to the ancient mill tenement. The stream, a man-made watercourse known as a leat, carried water to power the wheel on the side of the building on the left. This building was the mill and mill-house and all around were buildings associated with the business of grinding corn.

From medieval times it was usual for each manor to have its own grist mill, to which all the people who worked on the manor would be required to bring their corn. Certainly, there has been a mill on this site for a very long time – it does not appear in the Domesday Survey but is recorded as far back as 1316. At an enquiry at Chagford on 20 May 1316 the Manor of Lustleigh was held to have a capital messuage, worth 5 shillings a year, various lands and woods, and two corn mills worth 40 shillings a year. The neighbouring Manor of Wreyland had no mill, but the Lustleigh mill was on the River Wrey close to Wreyland. Documents of 1522, 1564 and 1566 refer to pieces of land in the Manor of Wreyland as Myllhill and Myllhill Close or Copse. Earlier, in 1437, a man was fined 12d. for hewing out millstones, and another man, John Caseley, was fined in 1478 for having again made a weir – perhaps for filling the leat to supply the Lustleigh mill.

From 1600 the mill is identified as being part of the Rudge estate in the Manor of Lustleigh, and continued to be so until 1961. In a survey of 1626 the 'mills tenement' is described as having an annual value of £2. The 'mills' here indicates two pairs of millstones working together. Theoretically, two pairs of stones would grind twice the amount of grain, and thus have twice the earning power of one pair and attract double the amount of rent.

Starting with the 1615 Wadham Survey of the Manor of Lustleigh it is possible to trace the names of all the millers from John Comyng and his son Cyprian to the Cousens family who worked here from the early-17th century to the mid-18th century. This period was the heyday of milling and the miller was often a powerful man locally; several members of the Cousens family served as churchwardens and waywardens. From 1743 the Cridford family leased the Mills for a decade or so until Thomas Hole is recorded in 1769 as being a churchwarden and living at the Mills. From then on, the Hole family worked here for the best part of 100 years.

The Tithe Map in 1837 showed the mill tenement as being held by William Hole; the 1841 population census states that he was aged 44 and living at the Mills with his wife Elizabeth and four children. In 1850, in *White's Directory*, this same William was described as a farmer and miller. According to the census of 1851 William and Elizabeth were still living at the Mills but there was no mention of the children; and in 1861 they were living at Mill Cottage a retired miller aged 64. Over the 100 years that the Hole family had lived at the Mills, we wonder which William Hole had scribbled his name in pencil on one of the bedroom walls.

From early times the mill at Bovey Tracey had a prescriptive right to grind the grist from all the tenements within the parish of Bovey Tracey. This meant that the inhabitants of the Manor of Wreyland were obliged to use the mill at Bovey Tracey rather than the much closer Lustleigh Mill. There was much resistance to this but a judgement at the Exchequer Chamber in 1732 upheld Bovey Tracey's right to the grinding of all the grist in the parish.

Suit of Mill was abolished in 1834 and after this the people of Wreyland were free to take their corn to Lustleigh Mill. But by the time the last of the Hole family had retired the fortunes of the mill were in decline. Milling continued but under a series of different names.

In order to improve the fortunes of the Mills, at some time during the early 1870s the bakery was built close to the mill building. In 1878 *White's Directory* describes George Endicott, living at the Mills, as baker and miller. He was still there in 1883 but by 1889 Samuel Dart had taken over. There is an entry in the *Parish Magazine* of 1891 which reads:

On Monday March 9th the snow which most people thought would not be seen again this winter, returned. On Tuesday March 10th many roads were impassable, a blizzard, that is a storm of wind and fine snow, raged for hours. Bread, through the bravery of bakers was supplied, and Mr. Dart and his man and boy happily live to tell the tale that they went from Lustleigh Mill to North Bovey, Barne and Peck with bags of loaves on their backs, and came back the same day.

Baking at the Mills continued throughout the First World War and into the early 1920s when the bakery at Brookfield took over. Milling continued sporadically at the Mills; the *Parish Magazine* in 1896 ran an article headed 'The Mill at work again' and the following year the *Directory* listed Richard Stoneman as watermiller and baker. However, this was the last mention in the *Directories* and the 1906 Ordnance Survey map described Lustleigh Mills as disused.

From the early years of the 20th century the mill house was rented out, and the mill machinery was still there and providing a wonderful but dangerous playground for the children who grew up at the property.

The mill-wheel sat quietly rotting away. In 1961 the Rudge estate was broken up by auction and the Mills went into private ownership. The first owner had the wheel dismantled and the machinery taken away for scrap. Subsequent owners gradually absorbed the milling premises in the main house. The Mill Leat remains, though seriously short of water in the summer months. It is an ever-present reminder of Lustleigh's industrial heritage.

❧ Chapter 4 ❧
DEFENCE OF THE REALM

THE HOME GUARD
by John Dray

Being a boy of only 14 when the war broke out in September 1939, I was like many of my friends, very excited, much I suppose, like the lads of a previous generation, who had flocked to the recruiting offices, to join in the great adventure that lay ahead. I had the previous year, when one summer evening a couple of khaki-painted lorries arrived in the village, with the purpose of recruiting the village lads to join the local Territorial Army unit of the 5th Devons, climbed the steps up to what was a mobile recruiting office. There were lots of posters adorning the walls, portraying soldiers marching through streets lined by pretty cheering young girls, and two real Vickers machine guns, with brass-buttoned soldiers explaining the wonders of their workings. I approached the waxed-moustached sergeant sitting at the table and asked to be enlisted. He asked my age and before I could answer, some wretched oaf behind me said 'he is only 13'. His war nearly came sooner than expected, but the kindly sergeant said to me, 'your time will come laddie' and I was to remember those words when I was trudging up through Italy as an infantry soldier some time later. I descended the steps, taking a last look at the cheering pretty girls and gave a loving touch to the mechanical wonder that could kill Germans in their thousands. I was deflated.

The Gould Platoon of the Junior Home Guard at Lower Hisley in 1943. Left to right: Jon, Hugh, Meg and Tony Gould.

Lustleigh Platoon of the Home Guard, under the command of Lt Jack Gould, in front of the Village Hall, c.1942. Seated, the Officers and NCOs, from left to right: Harold Olding, Mr Stock, Mr Farrell, Jack Gould (OC), Mr Laxton, Ernest Olding, Ernest Squires, Richard Bourne.

Later, in 1940, when it was announced a home defence army was to be formed, comprising mainly men too old and boys too young to join the regular Army, I thought that's for me, and once again queued to offer my services. Imagine my feelings, when once again being told I was too young and it would be better I tried the ARP (Air Raid Precautions) mob, ugh! ME pumping a blessed stirrup pump. I found it hard to believe they had turned me down, after all I had smoked a fag and shot a rabbit with a 12-bore.

Time passed by and the LDV (Local Defence Volunteers) were formed, Lustleigh raising quite a large force, among them my brother Ronald, soon to join the Army, but keen to get a bit of military experience while waiting. At that time there were no rifles or other weapons for them to practise with, but a number of owners of shotguns shared them, to give the appearance of some sort of military formation. The uniform in the early days was a khaki armband with large black letters LDV thereon. There was little they could do to express their readiness to repel an invader, but they did start a guard roster, by which two men were to stand guard of the telephone exchange, smaller then than now.

To provide shelter for the guards, a small wooden shed was built just inside the gate. We boys soon learnt that the guards would sometimes fall asleep, especially if they had partaken of a wee drop of 'rough' in the Cleave before reporting for their guard duty. It was while discussing this together with other village lads that I suggested we try and capture the exchange for a bit of a lark. Without going into too much detail and to cut the story short, we crept up close and when I gave the signal, we rushed in, slammed the door shut and locked it. Threats came from within, but I was basking in my sunshine, I had led and captured the exchange. My second in command, one Charlie Keenan, a full-blooded London Irish lad, whose family had arrived in the village as evacuees, got very excited and wanted to set fire to the whole caboodle and I had a job to restrain him. I 'withdrew my troops according to plan' as the BBC would announce whenever our troops had to disengage and withdraw.

Alas, there was a traitor in my Commando, and the next day a number of us were informed by the village 'bobby' that we were to report at the Village Hall the following evening on serious business. We duly arrived at the Hall, full of apprehension, with the word Borstal running through our heads. We were led in where sat the CO, a sergeant each side, the policeman also in attendance, all looking very stern. We were told how foolish our stunt had been and how we could have been shot and how we could be sent away (thoughts [were] 'Borstal here we come'), etc., etc.

Then, half impudently, half innocently, I asked what the public would think if they knew that a few young boys could outwit the custodians of their safety let alone a party of well-trained German soldiers. It nearly caused convulsions and we were told to get out, with more dire threats following us.

Sad really, I had let my family down, as only a short time before when my brother was a member of the LDV, his turn for guard duty had come around, but he was unable to do it having injured his leg in a motorcycle accident. It so happened my eldest brother George, who was serving in the Royal Artillery, had just arrived home from Dunkirk a few days before, but in spite of that, he had voluntarily done Ron's guard duty for him. It was much appreciated and a letter expressing appreciation arrived for my mother from the Commanding Officer.

Time went by and the LDV became the Home Guard; battledress uniforms, rifles and packs were issued. They were then becoming more like real soldiers. Here I must be serious. These men, true, because of age and work weariness, did look a little like characters from 'Dads' Army,' but on many of their chests were worn the ribbons of the medals awarded for service on the battlefields of the Somme, Ypres and Gallipoli, where the most terrible war of all time was fought, and this I respect to this day.

A rifle range was built in the field entered by a short grass lane opposite Caseley Court, the range facing toward the hill behind. To give warning when firing was in progress, a flagpole was installed high up on the hilltop. This was approached across the fields from the Mapstone Hill road at Bonwycks, then Sun Hill. Living at Higher Coombe at that time was a Captain Stephens, an ex-regular-Army officer, who had served in the Boer War as a sergeant with the Imperial Yeomanry, later to be a 'red tabbed' staff officer serving at Gallipoli and on the Western Front. As he lived close to the flagpole, he was asked to fly the red flag when live firing was to take place. Amusing, a member of the 'landed gentry' flying a red flag, but I joke. He agreed and was given a uniform which he never wore, but his request to be given the rank of CORPORAL – two stripes – was granted and there was one happy Capt. Stephens. Why? Because, as he declared, it was the only rank in the Army under that of Captain he had never held. He and I then came to an arrangement; that if he was for any reason unable to get to fly the flag I would do it for him. So you see, my day had come, I became second in command of flag-flying operations.

As the dark clouds still hung over the country, more thought was given to home defence and the Lustleigh Home Guard decided to set up road obstructions, installed at strategic places on each approach to the village. These were made up of portable obstructions such as large poles, rocks or whatever was near at hand. One such site was planned near Higher Coombe Gate and in order to have further defensive weapons handy, a small wooden shed was installed just inside the Cross field nearby. In this were kept a number of milk crates full of ready-to-use Molotov cocktails, an anti-tank inflammatory hand grenade – a grand name but they were only bottles filled with a mixture of petrol and tar with a piece of hessian cloth attached to the neck, which would be lit and the bottle hurled at the target, whereupon the bottle broke and the contents exploded. One German tank kaput.

The shed was locked with a sixpenny Woolworths padlock, the key being hidden in the wall against which the shed stood. My beady eye soon found that and one day a friend and I could not withstand the temptation and we stole one of the famous grenades. We took it to a quiet place and, after some hesitation, my friend lit the hessian and I hurled the bottle away. Not much of a bang but a bit frightening at first, a lot of flame and smoke, but [this] soon died down and there were no repercussions such as those that followed our first escapade.

At the age of just 16 and a month I went into the Army after again telling a white lie regarding my age; my time had come. The Home Guard continued to parade and drill in the road running down to the village orchard – no cars blocking it and no tar macadam, hard gravel in those days.

I may have sounded a little frivolous with my story, but I give all credit to those men of the Home Guard, who after a hard day's work turned out at any time of day or night to fulfil their duties and without a doubt gave comfort and morale, giving boost to our nation in those dark days – great men of a great generation. I am proud to have known them.

Above:
On parade in the winter of 1941/2.

Right: *The Platoon at the range at Rockvale.*

ROYAL BRITISH LEGION
by Christopher Jones

There is reasonable evidence that the Lustleigh Branch of the RBL was probably first formed in 1922 but all the early records have been lost and reliable information from the Branch minute-books does not begin until 1926 so this has now been formally adopted as the official formation date. At that time the President was Colonel Dunlop, the Chairman Mr Scott Painter (of the Cleave Hotel). The Treasurer was Mr A. Vanstone (headmaster of Lustleigh School) and the Secretary was Mr R. Dunlop. Committee members were Mr A.J. Horrell, Mr C. Bowden, Mr L. Hill, Mr P. Bunclarke, Mr W. Weeks, Mr A.J. Allin, Mr T. Coles, Mr R. Bowne and Mr W. Bray. The Relief Committee comprised Major General W.J. Fawcett (Chairman), Brigadier General W. Bland (Vice-Chairman), Mr Scott Painter (Treasurer), Mr R. Dunlop (Secretary) and members were Mr A. Chudley, Mr T. Coles and Miss Edwards.

At this time Mr Vanstone arranged for school-girls to be janitors to the war memorial and in recognition of this the Branch gave a gift at the end of the academic year. In 1926 it was found that the war memorial was incorrect and the name of Mr H.E. Smith was added to the tablet. In 1929 the Branch undertook a fund-raising card dance. The proceeds purchased a Standard for the Branch and its first Standard Bearer was Mr J. Bunclarke (senr).

In 1930 under the guidance of General Fawcett, the Branch organised a tea for members' children, which was held at his home, St Andrews. Such was the success that Christmas parties became an annual occurrence until the early 1960s. At that time the Branch was informed by its headquarters that it was outside its charity status to give help to the children in this way and, therefore, through the instigation of the Chairman, a new organisation was formed called the 'Lustleigh Christmas Party and Pantomime Committee', which continued for many years.

By 1940 with the commencement of the Second World War a period of change within the Branch occurred with many of its members rejoining the Armed Forces and from 1943 until early 1946 the Branch was held in abeyance. With the re-starting of the Branch at the end of the war many ex-servicemen came or returned to the village and new blood was introduced. Mr Mark Germon joined the committee and remained an integral part of it for the next 40 years. And, maintaining the family tradition, his son Douglas is now a committee member and has himself already served for 46 years. Among those returning was Dave Williams, who was elected to the committee in 1947 and served for the next 54 years as a committee member, as Chairman, and, in recent years, as President.

At this time the Branch had 153 members and special classes were held at the Horticultural Show solely for Legion members. A darts club was formed, competitions were entered and in its first year the club entered the South-Western Counties Darts Competition. In round one Lustleigh drew Branscombe. Branscombe complained that it was too far to travel to Lustleigh and withdrew giving Lustleigh a bye. In round two Lustleigh drew Chagford. The match held at the Cleave Hotel was

Dedication of Lustleigh War Memorial at the foot of Mapstone Hill in 1922.

General Fawcett of St Andrew's hands over the title to the war memorial ground which he had given to the Lustleigh Branch, here represented by Colonel Dunlop, July 1932.

won by Lustleigh 2-1. In rounds 3, 4 and 5 Lustleigh again received byes which resulted in the branch reaching the Devon Final having played only one match! However, the Devon final went the way of so many other matches; they received yet another bye and went through to the Devon and Cornwall final. This was held at Crownhill in Plymouth against St Austell from Cornwall. A 32-seater coach took the supporters to the match, which they successfully won 2-1. Lustleigh, therefore, progressed to the Grand Final held at Taunton where they played Chisledon from Wiltshire. Unfortunately, after an interesting experience, the team lost 2-1.

In 1948, on 13 November the war memorial was re-dedicated and 60 members under the command of Rear Admiral E.H. Drayson, CB, OBE, RN (Rtd), paraded. The re-dedication was undertaken by the Bishop of Crediton and the memorial was unveiled by Major General D.T. Cowan, CB, CBE, DSO, MC.

As a fund-raising event, the Branch held skittles competitions in the cricket field over a five-night period. In 1949, the low number of entries made was a disappointment to the Committee as many more were anticipated. The reason for the disappointing entry was that with the competition being in September the competition clashed with the hay harvest.

British Legion darts competitions faded away due to lack of numbers and the Lustleigh British Legion Darts Club became the Lustleigh Darts Club. And in consequence, the Walmsley Cup, previously owned by the British Legion, was transferred to the Darts Club in 1950.

A Women's Section of the British Legion was formed in 1951 by Mrs Winifred Horrell and played an important role until, due to a lack of ladies willing to form a committee, it disbanded in 1962. In 1964 it was agreed that water should be laid on to the war memorial to assist those who arranged the flower displays. The cost of this was agreed, but the pipes were not installed until 1971.

Over the years the Branch has assisted in many communal events, such as the Jubilee celebrations in 1935, the Coronation in 1952, the Silver Jubilee in 1977 and VE Day 50th anniversary in 1995. In addition a bench was placed in the Town Orchard in 1999 in memory of Mrs Beatrice Symes, who, although not a member, was a generous benefactor to the Branch.

The year 2001 saw the 75th anniversary and this was celebrated on Saturday 4 August with a truly memorable luncheon in the Village Hall for 60 members, wives and guests.

Chapter 5

THE COMMUNITY
AT WORK & AT PLAY

LUSTLEIGH PARISH COUNCIL
by Audrey Jenkins

In 1894 a meeting was held in the school with the rector in the Chair, to consider the Parochial Councils' Act (c.1893). The rector was anxious that goodwill should prevail and that all should try and make the Act successful. The expenses of Parish Meetings and elections were to be paid out of the Poor Rate. The first meeting to form a Parish Council for Lustleigh was called by a notice dated 24 November 1894 which stated that there were to be seven councillors who would be elected from candidates nominated by a proposer and a seconder. It was to be held at the School Room on 4 December 1894 at 6.30 in the evening.

On the due date the Reverend Henry Tudor was elected Chairman of the meeting and 18 nominees were named – one withdrew his name and an election was held. Those elected were: Frederick Amery, William Bartlett, Ranulph Edward Glanville, Edwin May, William Nicholls, John Raymont and William Wills. It was proposed, seconded and passed unanimously that the Reverend H. Tudor be elected Chairman of the Parish Council, although, strangely, he was not a councillor!

Charles Sumpter Amery was elected to the post of Clerk of the Parish Council – his remuneration to be decided at a later date, and Mr T.M. Hoskin, a bank employee, was appointed Treasurer of the Council. He was to give security in the amount of £50 which was subsequently placed with the Capital and Counties Bank in Newton Abbot. In due course the Clerk was awarded £5 per annum – to Lady Day 1896. A Mr C. Sampson was to be paid 2s.0d. a night for 'light and firing' for Council meetings.

At the Annual Parish Assembly in April 1895 Messrs Wills of Eastwrey, Glanville of Ellimore, Harvey of Fursden and Bartlett of the Post Office were appointed Overseers of the Council and an Assistant Overseer was to be appointed for collecting the Sanitary Rate for the Sanitary Board. A precept of £4 was agreed and was paid to the Overseers to be managed by them, and at this time (1896) the adult population of Lustleigh was 399.

In 1898 the precept rose to £6. In this year it was recorded that all parochial electors, women included, married or single, were entitled to vote. The Parish Council requested the local County Councillor to use his influence to have Lustleigh constituted a separate Polling District. Very little money was spent by the Council at this time – a few shillings for a year's lighting and cleaning of the meeting room, horse labour cost 11s.0d. a year, and five days' work on Wreyland footpath during the year cost 3s.0d a day. Other expenses were for stationery and postage.

In October 1898 the Clerk was instructed to write to the Superintendent of Police calling his attention to the dangerous practice of lighting bonfires in the village on 5 November and asking him to take suitable steps to prevent such proceedings! The Clerk was also instructed to write to the local Government Board advising that body that a sore throat of a Diphtheric type existed in Wreyland (one had earlier proved fatal and the Board School had already been closed) and to request that the Board consider the water scheme urgently.

A Footpath Committee was set up by the Council specifically for reporting on Wreyland Path. The path under the bridge was giving much concern and it was agreed that posts should be erected on both sides of the railway bridge to prevent the passage of horses and cattle – one on the Wreyland side and two on the village side – at a cost of 12s.0d.

In 1899 the Annual Parish Assembly voted to ask the Great Western Railway to provide more facilities for 'sending away horses, cattle, carriages and furniture vans'. Much consideration was given at this time to the acquiring of land for allotments, but landlords were consistently reluctant to make land available for this purpose.

In 1900 the Reverend Henry Tudor was still being elected Chairman for the year – although still not a councillor, but in 1904 a councillor was elected to be the Chairman and the name of the Reverend Henry Tudor ceased to appear again in the records.

However, in 1907, Mr Cecil Torr was elected to Chair the Annual Parish Assembly although he was not a councillor. In this year footpaths continued to be a problem, not only Wreyland (for which Bovey Tracey Council was by now being asked to make a

The road by the Wrey Brook and the Mill Leat. Cleaning out of the Leat is one of
the perennial problems which has repeatedly been discussed at Parish Council meetings.

financial contribution for repairs – as were the house residents), but also to Pethybridge, Higher Coombe, Peck Farm and Foxworthy. In 1912 the Council made a (successful) request for a Sunday service of trains.

During the First World War the Council concerned itself with studying the many documents issued by the War Office and set up a National War Savings Scheme. One of the continuing concerns was the storage for fire hoses which culminated in them being stored in the Old Vestry. By virtue of the Small Holdings and Allotments Act the Parish Council was required to register the details of the allotments in the parish. At this time seven people urgently required an allotment, but still no suitable land had been found; landowners continued to squabble among themselves and the Council continued to search.

Regrettably, there are no recorded Parish Council minutes available between 1915 and 1954. If any reader has any knowledge of the whereabouts of such papers the current Parish Council would be very grateful to be advised.

Throughout 1955 the subject discussed at most Council meetings was the Village Green – posing an ongoing problem because of docks, thistles, nettles and the like, but it was not until 2 December 1955 that a public meeting was held to discuss the plans which had been drawn up for improvement. It is recorded that between 80 and 90 villagers attended and, according to all accounts, it was a lively meeting! However, an amendment to the proposed plans, calling for 'no action to be taken for 12 months, during which time tidying and digging-up of nettles and some grasses should be undertaken by paid and voluntary labour' was adopted. A 'litter-picker' was employed at 7s.6d. a week.

Mr Barlow, the owner of Primrose Café, was in trouble for encroaching onto the Village Green by making a flower bed and path outside his entrance gate! The Council also wrote several times to Mr Allan of Little Holne (?) asking him to remove a pile of earth and building materials left on the Green after laying his water main. Two years later, through 1958 and 1959, the Green was still being kept tidy (and trees were being pruned by Mr Harvey) and so it seems that it is thanks to the consistent hard work at that time there is a pleasant Village Green in the year 2001.

Over the following years and with persistent pressure the Parish Council seems to have been responsible for the introduction of dust-bin collections, the removal of refuse tips, the inclusion of Wreyland and Brookfield into the parish, the supply of bins for salt, sand and gravel (formerly 'heaps'), buses into the village rather than passing by along the main road, and the installation of the bus shelter at St Andrew's Corner – among many other things which now are taken for granted.

More than 100 years have passed since the formation of the Parish Council (the electoral roll now has 511 names on it) and some problems have remained much the same throughout that time – repairs to Wreyland Path, cleaning out of the Leat, worries about footpaths... and pot-holes... and overgrown hedges, the managing of the Town Orchard and its trees and the maintenance of the Village Green, although in modern times we seldom, if ever, have to write to the occupiers of properties drawing their attention to the dilapidation of their homes!

SOME MEMORIES OF LUSTLEIGH SCHOOL
by Hugh Gould

In 1876 the old Dame and her pupils moved from the original school, 'built by subscription and endowed with Lowton Meadow in Moreton for supporting a school for ever by Revd William Davy...' They moved into the new school, built by the School Board under the provisions of the 1870 Education Act. The earliest memory of the school available in the Lustleigh archives is recorded in a letter written to a newspaper in 1960 when the school was threatened with closure. Mr J.D. Livingstone remembers it with affection and sends a photograph of 26 boys, comprising the boys' section of the upper school in 1898. Mr L. Sing was the headmaster, from whom he received, in 1899 or 1900, a 'never absent or never late' medal.

Still living in the village today are Joan Ellis, John Dray, and Bill and Nell Squires, and I am indebted to them for their memories of the school in the late 1920s and the 1930s. Bill went there at the age of five in 1927. Joan too went that year, but she was only three and a half years old. She very much wanted to go to school and always loved it. There were at least 80 children in the school at that time, which was divided into three classes: the infants were taught by Miss Bennett – Bill remembers her as a rotund lady with one good eye; the juniors, divided into standards 1, 2 and 3, were taught by Miss Brinicombe, a very nice lady, Joan remembers, who came each day by train from Newton Abbot; and the seniors, divided into standards 4, 5, 6 and 7, were taught by the headteacher, Mr Vanstone. Nell, then a Wills from Higher Hisley, came to the school the following year. She was later sent to be privately educated at Hingston Convent near Newton Abbot. Bill and Nell were to marry in 1944.

Bill remembered Lustleigh School providing a very good education, but he told me that Mr Vanstone could be easily distracted by being asked about India, where he had served during the First World War. In those inter-war years Empire Day was an important festival when the schoolchildren sang 'Land of Hope and Glory'. Joan also remembered good educational standards. The 1930s were years of depression, and many of the Lustleigh children were poor.

Some were malnourished and suffered from rickets. However, some children walked every day all the way from Tottiford Reservoir! In the winter they were allowed to leave half an hour early in order to get home before dark. The school had a cupboard of spare clothing for these children and others like them who had walked from outlying areas through the rain to class. There was a dread of polio, and two children died of it. Joan told me that the school was closed for three weeks to try to prevent the spread of the disease.

Outside lessons the children worked hard and played hard. They looked forward to the school's annual outing, usually to Teignmouth, and a free tea. Major Burton, at Lustleigh Manor, gave an annual children's party and presents. His two daughters were Sunday-school teachers. Bill had to deliver milk in the morning to 14 houses before going to school, and his 'pay' was two pints of skimmed milk for his mother!

The May Day practices were held at school and the maypole dancing thoroughly rehearsed. There was no running round the maypole; the children were expected to dance. Joan told me that one punishment was not to be allowed to take part in the May Day practice; it was a great deprivation because all the children wanted to be involved.

John remembered the games the boys played: they bartered for cigarette cards and played with spinning tops which they had made themselves using cotton reels and wooden meat skewers and leather bootlaces. They jousted with conkers in season. The girls played hopscotch. The hunt used to meet on the Village Green two or three times a year, and the children's break was extended so that they could watch from the school yard. Miss Bennett played the piano to entertain the children on wet days, and Mr Vanstone would supervise them in country dancing. Mr Reeves, Mr Vanstone's successor, introduced woodwork classes in Lustleigh, using oak offcuts from coffins, and the boys did not want to touch this wood! The boys gardened plots in the field across the road, and each plot had a big boy and a little one responsible for its upkeep. The tools were kept in a shed and cleaned and oiled on wet days.

The school leaving age was then 14. When boys reached that age and left school, their parents would buy them their first pair of long trousers, a significant rite of passage. John said that most children, on leaving school, found work in Lustleigh.

Bill Saunders went to Lustleigh School, aged five, after the Easter holiday in 1940, and he

Joy Kitson joins the hunt on her pony at a meet on the Green in the 1930s.

A school group in 1904. The schoolmaster, Mr T.W. Williamson, stands at the back.

The following faces from this school group from c.1937 were identified by Joan Ellis (née Bourne). Left to right, back row: Ernest Tremlett, John Harvey, David Allin, Irene Dray, Iris Bowden, Arthur Horrell, Sonny Orsman, Godfrey Lockyer; 3rd row: Joan Bourne (now Ellis), Joyce Horrell, Hazel Phillips, Dorothy Allin, Marjorie Germon, Jennifer Retter, Jose Amery, Phyllis Wills, Winifred Olding; 2nd row (kneeling): Dudley Retter, Sylvia May, Betty Bowden, Edna Dray, Pamela Wills, Joyce Holloway, Andrew Retter; front: William (Bill) Amery, Desmond Waldron, Francis Amery, Lionel Orsman, Kenneth Germon.

remained there until 1948, when it closed as a senior school. That year the school leaving age was raised to 15, and those over 11 years old went on to Highweek School in Newton Abbot, to separate schools for boys and for girls. Bill went there for one term only, the summer term. He went in September to South Devon Technical College, eventually becoming an engineer running his own business in Birmingham. When he started school in 1940, he had to walk every day the two and a half miles from Higher Elsford.

In the autumn term of that year the evacuees arrived and the numbers in the school greatly increased to a maximum of 140 in late 1940. The infants were moved to Church House, where all the others joined them for lunch. Mrs Wills, Margaret Jones' mother, was the cook. Previously children had brought their own lunch, often an egg, which was put into a wicker basket and marked with the child's name. The school only supplied milk, and George Amery's father, Fred, had the milk round. In winter every child brought a piece of wood to keep the stove burning or there would not have been enough fuel. These pieces of wood were put into an old tea chest.

During the war the headteacher seems to have been responsible for measuring the children's feet to see if they qualified for extra clothing coupons, and for dishing out egg powder, from Canada, and chocolate powder for drinking. The children were encouraged to collect rosehips, which were sent away for turning into rosehip syrup.

When Bill arrived at the school Mr Reeves was the headteacher, but he soon left to join the RAF. There was then a succession of supply teachers – Bill remembers one who could not keep order and an evacuee boy breaking the school cane! In 1942 Mr Collier came and stayed throughout the war and after it. He was very much in control and achieved high standards. He was a good teacher and a high percentage of pupils passed the 11-plus exam. The Local Education Authority apparently used to claim that the children came from privileged backgrounds but, in most cases, it was not true. The more privileged children in Lustleigh were privately educated.

In the big classroom, the senior children sat in three rows of desks, each row representing a different age group. They sat in their rows according to their size, the smallest at the front

School group, c.1936. Left to right, back row: ?, Kenneth Germon, John Harvey, Sonny Orsman, Dudley Retter, David Allin, Peter Horrell; middle: Walter Osborne, Jennifer Retter, Dorothy Allin, Rhona Lake, Marjorie Germon, Joan Bourne (with doll), Joyce Horrell (also with doll), Mary Hicks, Sylvia May, Kathleen Bourne, John Horrell; front: Bill Amery, Andrew Retter, Lionel Orsman.

ranging to the largest at the back. Mr Collier had a blackboard on wheels and taught a row at a time.

The children gardened in the field opposite the school, the boys growing vegetables and the girls flowers. Mr Collier was very keen on cricket. He used to get six boys to pull the roller to prepare the village cricket pitch. He later needed eight boys when the school no longer had seniors! On Friday mornings the older pupils went on the train to Bovey, the girls to be taught cooking and the boys woodwork. The annual outing to Teignmouth or Paignton still took place. Bill learned to swim on one such trip.

At Lustleigh, as opposed to Wreyland, children received annually 17s.6d. from the Davy Trust, but only if they had a full attendance record and had not been late! It was presented by the rector, then Robert Ryder, at the end of the summer term. There was a Scout troop, a boys' cricket team and Mr Collier ran a youth club boasting table tennis and a three-quarter-size billiard table.

The great snows of 1947 closed the school for three weeks and there were no trains for six weeks. There were only eleven children at the school at that time. Three boys were sent to help Mr George Reed with the milk round. The other three boys went to Mr Osborne to help him deliver bread. Three girls were sent to Mr Bibbings, the grocer. The remaining two children were too young to be put to work. The

rector, Canon Newman, skied to Moreton for meat. The *Herald Express* recorded the school closure in 1963, the petition against which was started by Mrs Edna Bowden, who collected 217 signatures. Sadly she could not prevent it. Mrs Margaret Mathews said at the time that the closing of the school would be like taking the life away from the village. There is no doubt that Lustleigh has changed a great deal.

Since 1989 the Church House has been a private village school (see page 49).

The 1876 board school building at Lustleigh, and (right) the dame school built by Parson Davy, which it replaced.

Lustleigh loses its village school after 139 years

By KATHLEEN FRENCH

ONLY for a little longer will the children of Lustleigh attend the village school there. Numbers have fallen and are unlikely to increase.

The closure of any village school is saddening; but at Lustleigh it brings to an end the story of education there which began in 1824. Under the eaves of a little granite building (now used as a surgery) on the west side of the churchyard is a simple inscription:

"1825 Built by subscription and endowed with Lowton Meadow in Moreton for supporting a school for ever by the Rev. William Davy, curate of this parish, upwards of forty years."

The photograph above shows the Old Vestry, the village school from 1825 to 1867. The picture on the left shows the School House, the village school from 1878 to 1963.

95

Lustleigh Village Hall

The opening ceremony on 1 October 1911. The Hall continued as the 'Constitutional Hall' certainly until after 1925, but later changed to the 'Conservative Hall'.

This is thought to be a photograph of a Christmas party in the Village Hall.

Repairs to the Village Hall, 1999

The retaining wall extends between the Village Hall and the Post Office. Postmaster Barry Marsh looks on.

Traffic mayhem at the church steps as heavy earth-moving equipment arrives.

The digger gets to work to hold back the threatening hillside.

The new retaining wall takes shape.

Concrete mix being delivered by overhead crane.

Almost finished, the retaining wall takes shape.

Beating the Bounds

Above: *Beating the bounds in 1924*
with the Revd Henry Johnson, rector.

Below and right: *Beating the bounds in 1924 .*

Beating the Bounds

Above: *Beating the bounds, 1924. Cecil Torr is centre and PC Albert Winser controls the throng.*

Below and right: *Beating the bounds, 1980.*

Village Events

Garden fête at Combe House, c.1921.

A village outing sets off in a charabanc in the early 1920s from Kelly Cross Cottage.

Village Events

Queen Victoria's Golden Jubilee is celebrated in the village.

A May Day audience in the Town Orchard (date unknown). Colonel Walmesley is in the foreground, left.

WOMEN'S INSTITUTE
by Audrey Jenkins

The Women's Institute is for all women, offering them opportunities for friendship and for learning and working together to improve the quality of life in the community, to enable development of individual skills and talents and opportunities to join in a wide range of WI activities. With well over a quarter of a million members it is the largest women's voluntary organisation in the United Kingdom. It is non-sectarian and non-party-political and has always been actively involved in the social, environmental and consumer issues of the day.

The WI tree begins with members and individual institutes, followed by Groups (four or five WIs which are geographically near each other), then by County Federations and finally is topped by the National Association. The National Federation of Women's Institutes is a constituent member of the Associated Country Women of the World (ACWW), an international organisation of more than eight million women. Members travelling abroad can, therefore, be put in touch with similar organisations through the ACWW.

Lustleigh WI was formed during the Second World War – in March 1941 – and so was 60 years old at the time of the publication of this book. During its first year 63 members were enrolled, each paying an annual subscription of two shillings. In 1942 72 members enrolled and in 1943 the membership rose to 84. In 1944 the subscription rose to 2s.6d. and in 1948 to 3s.6d. Some of those members' names are still known in the village – among them Amery, Bloomer, Ellis, Gould, Squires and Wills. Indeed, Mrs Beryl Gould, now living in the Old School House, was a founder member.

At this time the Village Hall was, in fact, the Conservative Hall and from records it would appear that, although the hall was used for WI meetings, no rent was paid by the WI for the use of the building for two years until a payment was introduced in 1943. In 1943, the hire of the hall for 'an event' cost £1.1s.0d. There must have been an open boiler in the hall at this time because records show that in 1945 a delivery of coal and coke cost 3s.11d. In 1946 the WI noticeboard was installed in the village at a cost of £2.0s.0d.

In 1949 the charge for teas at meetings was raised from 2d. to 3d. (in 2001 it is 30p, equivalent to 6s.0d.). On one occasion, when the water heater failed, helpers carried teapots over from the shop.

Lustleigh Women's Institute in the Village Hall, 1965. The President, Claire Harris, is seated fifth from the right. On her right is Mrs Coles and on her left is Joan Raikes.

The WI in a more relaxed mood, dancing the conga.

Today's members should remember that – just in case...! The Food Office had to issue a licence to enable the WI to purchase tea and sugar as many items of food were still rationed at this time. Members donated 'eats' for teas at meetings. Also at this time, a food parcel received from the Country Women's Association of New South Wales in Australia was raffled and eight lucky members went home clutching goodies. Prizes at meetings, for one competition or another, frequently included bottles of fruit, or a parcel of tea and sometimes eggs. On one occasion 26 members played whist at a Group whist drive!

Throughout the 1940s and '50s there were many members' outings, exhibitions, demonstrations, children's parties, pensioners' outings, 'help-each-other' classes (including upholstery), dress-making classes and Group meetings with neighbouring WIs.

In the 1950s the Committee met at the Post Office and in 1951 the WI acquired its own crockery cupboard – thankfully it seems – for others were using, and sometimes breaking, items 'borrowed'.

In 1952 bring-and-buy stalls were held at meetings to raise funds for the Christmas Party for 'the old folks', a concert was held to raise funds (£9.9s.0d.) for Lynmouth WI to help them after the terrible floods of that year and carol singers sent £6.0s.0d. to The Blind of Devon. Also in 1952 the President made a presentation to a member who, 'for

a long time has done so much back-room work at meetings', a pair of warm blue slippers – hand-made, naturally!

In 1959 a WI choir was formed and in the 1950s and '60s silver spoons were given to the new babies of members. At this time Lustleigh WI had a number of musicians in its membership: there were several pianists, more than one violinist and an accordianist. (In 2001 there is only one member who admits to being a musician – a pianist – and who, consequently, has many demands made upon her.)

In 1965, Golden Jubilee year of the first WI in the United Kingdom, one member from every WI was invited to a garden party at Buckingham Palace and so a ballot was held. Lustleigh WI had a grand Jubilee Exhibition in the village in September of that year and a garden party was held in the Orchard. A Borneo hardwood seat with bronze plaque was donated to the village: even then it was suggested that the seat be bolted to its base! In this year there were 89 members, with a committee of 13 and the choir won several awards at an Exeter Musical Festival.

In 1967 the bursary to enable members to attend a course at Denman College (the WI Education Centre in Berkshire) was increased from £10 to £15 and every year in the '60s there were so many members wishing to attend that a ballot had to take place.

During the 1960s an active Drama Group produced plays and pantomimes for the village and at this time potential members were still having to be proposed and seconded for membership before being allowed to become a WI member. In the 1960s and early '70s WI meetings were held in the afternoons (once a month) between September and April, but in May, June and July they were held in the evenings. In April 1971 the roof of the Conservative Hall was to be repaired, so the April meeting had to be held in the evening and the WI agreed to help at a fête in order to raise more funds for the re-roofing work.

In 1971 the cost of hiring a coach to take members to the Devon County Show was 25p per person (we were into the new currency by then). In 1974 there were still 89 members, but fuel restrictions were still in force and in December the party – with senior citizens as guests – had to be cancelled. In 1975 concern was expressed by some members at the cutting-down of 'well-known and beautiful trees' and it was suggested that members should seek preservation orders for trees which enhanced the village. In 1976 the WI reluctantly paid £10 to the Parish Council for a timber tree protector. Three new trees had been planted in the Orchard, two provided by the Parish Council and one by the WI, and it was considered essential that they should be protected.

In 1978 a Lustleigh WI member became the County Scrabble Champion and also a runner-up in the County Driver of the Year competition; in the same year a member became 4th in the Gardeners' Brain of Britain competition.

By the mid 1980s membership had dropped to 65. In May 1988 the WI approached the Parish Council with its concerns about dog-fouling on the Village Green and a number of members volunteered to help with a regular Sunday canteen for families visiting prisoners at Channings Wood Prison.

On to the 1990s when meetings, classes and tea-parties were held from time to time in the building now known as the Garden House, at Yonder Wreyland – and membership numbered approximately 50. In the year 1991 came the 50th birthday when all members were presented with an engraved champagne flute, crocuses were planted around the outside of the churchyard wall and apple trees were bought for the orchard.

At this time the WI became a shareholder in the village photocopier which enabled participating organisations and their members to have copies at cost price. It was housed for several years in the Old Vestry and then moved to the Post Office when the postmaster agreed to make required photocopies, thereby improving the service – the Post Office being open more regularly than the Old Vestry. Ten years later this service still exists.

Experience of committee work, public speaking and insight into pressing social and environmental issues lead many members to stand for local councils. In 1949 two WI members were elected to the Parish Council; other members have served on the Council over the years and in 2001 there were three WI members on the Lustleigh Parish Council. This time the number of members stood at 36 and the annual subscription was £16.25p.

LUSTLEIGH DRAMA GROUP
by Janet Power in collaboration with Jennie Powys

In many towns and villages, drama groups abound, such is the attraction of plays and the desire to act in them. However, did many begin in as colourful a way as our own theatricals here in Lustleigh?

In those early days, the word 'drama' seems to have been synonymous with the name Gould. We are indebted to the late Iris Gould for the gift to the archives of the first album holding details of the thespian activities inspired by her husband's uncle, James Nutcombe Gould, who, with his large family, lived at Knowle. According to Iris' beautiful handwritten introduction, James, who was a friend of the famous Henry Irving, was a talented amateur actor and he obviously master-minded the formation of the group of enthusiastic players, several from his own family, who performed in the Revd Frederic Ensor's barn at The Manor. It appears that this barn became a small well-patronized theatre and the actors formed themselves into 'The Barn Owls', their first programme in the album being dated 1879. What local excitement it must have caused! A newspaper cutting from that time reads:

An amateur theatrical performance far up on the Dartmoor range is indeed a novelty. The performance took place last week in a barn at Lustleigh, and of course all the people of the surrounding district were there.

In the next extract Mr J.N. Gould is described as 'the pervading spirit' and so he must have been. The productions appear to have come thick and fast, the first, presumably, of two one-act plays, *A Phenomenon in a Smock Frock* and *Little Toddlekins*.

All programmes from these early days note the good cause supported by each production. Could that have been the original motivation behind the formation of The Barn Owls – putting to good use the theatrical talents of this prodigious group of family and friends? Especially as the first performance was 'in aid of the Widows and Orphans of soldiers who have fallen in the War in South Africa'. Money was then raised for the fund for 'warming the parish Church' and the 'Atalanta' fund, another piece of tantalising history unknown to this writer. But the paramount ongoing fund-raiser was the church organ fund.

Performances became more ambitious, culminating in *The Merchant of Venice* in 1883. This resulted in huge press coverage! Three long columns were assigned to this epic by a pen largely dipped in vinegar! Indeed, so sparing in his praise was this one critic who signed himself 'Aficionado', that two readers, neither of whom had Lustleigh connections, wrote in to castigate him for his ill temper and lack of charity for the worthy players. All his malice was turned on its head, however, by another serious reviewer, who wrote of splendid dresses, pretty scenery and 'beautiful elocution'. The same goes on to praise the whole piece, where there was no hitch from beginning to end! The newspaper cuttings are in fact a delight and make very entertaining and informative reading. It must be said that Aficionado himself writes memorably about the barn experience. His reference to the 'dramatically disturbed pig', heard, uninvited, in the background, is one of his more lovable offerings.

A less demanding production was a scene from *The Taming of the Shrew*, which was actually presented at the Dolphin Hotel, Bovey Tracey. Having commended Mr J.N. Gould and his supporting actors, the list of audience then predominates. It included the Duke and Duchess of Somerset, the Dowager Lady Morley, Sir Samuel and Lady Baker, and Lord Exmouth. One wonders if the Dolphin Hotel was a suitably more genteel auditorium than the barn for these local representatives of the aristocracy. Certainly they were being asked to contribute to the on-going organ fund!

In January 1882, large print proclaimed that *The Merchant of Venice* would be produced during the Easter holidays. In fact, *The Merchant* did not appear until a year later in January 1883. It gives comfort to present-day directors to realise that even the talented, versatile Barn Owls sometimes ran into areas of difficulty serious enough to force a postponement!

There is a particularly endearing entry at the beginning of the album, where a member of the Company – maybe James himself – pays tribute to their prompter, by way of a poem which ends with the lines: 'Our helm, our compass, and our guide'. This is addressed to 'Katherine', and leaves one wishing so very much to know who she was.

The last record of these wonderful early productions is that of 1883. James Nutcombe Gould's photograph, the first entry in the album, appropriately presides over this fascinating history. Other family photographs are also included. Of course there is a reminder of this inspiring actor every time one walks across the Green and passes the church. The Gould Memorial Lantern was erected in 1899 to commemorate the life of James and his wife Edith, and according to Iris, 'to provide light in the centre of the Village' *(see also pages 43 and 141)*.

The 'Goulden' era was not yet over. Between the wars, the Lustleigh Dramatic Society was formed

James Nutcombe Gould, founder of The Barn Owls, 1879.

by the Gould brothers, Arthur, husband of Iris, and Jack, husband of Beryl. Sadly, there are no photographs or programmes in the archives relating to this period, but Iris' notes tell us that the society flourished.

After the intervening Second World War, a new society came into being in 1945 – 'The Lustleigh Players'. Never ones to duck a challenge, their first production was *Pygmalion* by George Bernard Shaw. As well as being the Chairman of this society, Arthur Gould appears on the programme as 'Sarcastic Bystander' and brother Jack has the starring role of Professor Higgins. New names appear as producers: Barbara Musgrave and Hilda Drayson. Miranda elicited a long and glowing press report, which praises the production as 'well acted, perfectly dressed, and meticulously produced' and ends with the words: 'Producer, and a good one too, was Hilda Drayson'.

A long list of plays performed during this period includes *When We Are Married* by J.B. Priestley, and *Blithe Spirit* by Nöel Coward. A nice touch in two of the programmes is the acknowledgement that the telephone was lent by the Postmaster General!

'Shakespere in the Orchard' present Winged Cupid, *summer 1975, with Mary Powys, Peter Hewison (in the basket) and Camilla Renwick.*

Sheila Manners as Princess Rosabelle and Jackie Kennett as Jack in Jack and the Beanstalk, New Year's Eve, 1976.

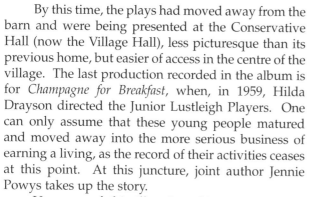

By this time, the plays had moved away from the barn and were being presented at the Conservative Hall (now the Village Hall), less picturesque than its previous home, but easier of access in the centre of the village. The last production recorded in the album is for *Champagne for Breakfast*, when, in 1959, Hilda Drayson directed the Junior Lustleigh Players. One can only assume that these young people matured and moved away into the more serious business of earning a living, as the record of their activities ceases at this point. At this juncture, joint author Jennie Powys takes up the story.

Unaware of this illustrious history, I came to Lustleigh in 1972 and found no drama group in existence. There was, however, a suitable cast for my favourite farce, *Wild Goose Chase*; rehearsals were well under way before we really noticed the absence of an officially-constituted society without which you cannot get insurance or procure a licence. The WI had kindly acted as our alma mater, but on 12 November 1973 at a public meeting at Church House the present Lustleigh Drama Group was founded. On 21 November the licence was obtained and the play was presented at the end of the month, right in the middle of the fuel crisis. We were not allowed to heat the hall and the audience braved the winter nights with rugs and hot-water bottles. This almost seemed to help us. *The Advertiser* headline was 'Audience warms to re-born group' and the *Parish Magazine* noted: 'The nights were cold but this amusing piece in which all the players seemed to be enjoying themselves too, warmed our hearts.'

Curiously the Drama Group also initiated something which has reverberated in the village ever since; buying a new curtain track for the hall, it was remarked that this was in effect a donation to the Conservative Association which then owned the building. The group was not supposed, of course, to have any political affiliations, so Ted Renwick, Group Secretary, commenced enquiries that eventually led to the hall being taken over by the Parish Council and becoming the Village Hall rather than the Conservative Hall.

In the first 12 months I directed three plays: the farce, a thriller and a Tom Stoppard play, *The Real Inspector Hound*. In this play the two main characters are drama critics who must appear to be sitting in the audience, so we performed in the round, with the audience sitting on the stage and around the sides of the acting area which was the middle of the hall. At the same time we were writing our first pantomime, *Dick Whittington*, which in January 1975 became our fourth production in 14 months, directed by Sandy Mason. The dame always carries a pantomime and Michael Price had no trouble doing so. The seats sold out and by now we had put our first £100 in the bank and over 100 adults and children on the stage.

The next summer Sandy's Shakespeare compilation *Winged Cupid* was performed in the Orchard – a halcyon summer when it seemed never to rain at all. Two one-act plays followed that autumn, *Forgotten Dreams* and *I Spy*, directed by Peter Mason and Peter Hewison respectively. Returning to farce once again drew in the audience the following year when Jane Jacobs directed Ben Travers' *Rookery Nook* to great acclaim, followed by another pantomime, this time *Jack and the Beanstalk*, presented at the turn of the year, again with delightful music by James Hooker and another brilliant dame in Mike Jacobs.

What energy we must all have had then to do so many things in so short a time. It was a very happy time and certain things stand out. In *Wild Goose Chase* there is a running joke of a batty member of the peerage trying to shoot the postman, who does not appear in the cast list. The village postman had for many years been Len Symes, a great character, whose unexpected appearance at the end of the play, determinedly following the fleeing peer across the stage with gun levelled, regularly brought the house down. A director doesn't have much to do once the play is in performance, but one of my tasks was to go out at 9.30 each evening and extract Len from the pub in time for his entrance.

A local drama group is all about having fun but there is a more serious side too. We took both our pantomimes, *Dick Whittington* and *Jack and the Beanstalk*, to the Hawkmoor Hospital and the Langdon Hospital, Dawlish, where the audience was quite difficult and the children managed so well we were really proud of them. And I was particularly pleased when a Parish Councillor (unnamed but recorded in the minutes) remarked after our first year, 'the village is mixing well as a community, due to the work of the Drama Group.' This had always been one of my main but secret aims.

The lighter side abounds. The group produced many excellent parties, perhaps responsible for a large ink blot in the minutes with an arrow to a small 'Sorry'. The writing of the two pantomimes with Bob Bickle, Mike Jacobs, Sandy Mason, Mike Price and Peter Hewison was fuelled with cider and was an amazing form of group therapy. All our best jokes ended up on the cutting-room floor – definitely actionable but privately so good for the soul.

Other hilarious moments included an actor who always tried to open stage doors the wrong way, practically demolishing the set and once in desperation exiting through the fireplace; and a wicked stage crew (could it have included Dave Wills?) who decided to deflate the ego of the stage manager by convincing him they had lost the Beanstalk on the way to the Hawkmoor (and how did they manage to hide something so big?).

A Saturday morning in the Orchard with the Junior Drama Club in 1984 and their show Contrasts. *Left to right, main row:* Tom Gould, Christopher Maynard, Jane Robertson, Roslyn Maynard, Rebecca Merriott, Vicky Parkin, James Mosely, Rebecca Parkin, Daniel Smith, Carolyn Tapson *and* Coralie Olver; *kneeling:* Tanya Lee *and* Oliver White. *At the back, left of tree is* Tim Parkin *and to the right of the tree are* Justin Lee *and* Virginia Tapson.

Jan Rowe in She Stoops to Conquer.

Programme for Dick Whittington, *1995.*

The magic of amateur drama, commented on by Bob Bickle, is the way the utter chaos of rehearsals is suddenly transformed when the scenery, the costumes and the lights, and – if you are lucky – the actors knowing their words, miraculously turn your ugly ducklings into the swan you had almost despaired of. The addictive experience is of everybody suddenly stopping their beefing and pulling together so well that for that short time it seems that everybody loves everybody. Where else can you get such laughter and true fellowship?

The best times come to an end. I left the Lustleigh area in 1978 to work at Dartington, and sadly for the group the Masons, Sandy and Peter, both professionally trained and very talented, left shortly afterwards. Rosemary Harthill, our Dick Whittington and often heard since on the BBC, had left a little earlier, and Jane Jacobs, another talented actress and director, also left the area. But phoenix like from the ashes the Drama Group rose again with a new cast of characters who have carried it onward to the present day. Janet Power resumes the narrative to bring the story up to date.

This new cast of Drama Group characters includes Erica and Leslie Read, whose stagecraft and acting skills were to play a major part in the fortunes of the group in the years to come, and in 1983 Will Carnell asked newcomer Janet Power to join him in a production of *The Beggar's Opera*. His adaptation of the music by John Gay and his talent as musical director assured success. Somehow he managed to persuade actors who had never sung to find their voices and the final outcome was a colourful show, full of vitality. He did the same for *Caucasian Chalk Circle* in 1987 with his own musical compositions. On both occasions a talented orchestra augmented the script. Both these productions involved so many actors, stage crew and musicians that they became as much village projects as dramatic productions. A never-to-be-forgotten moment was when a little flurry in the orchestra occurred, involving a change of costume among the violins. Out from the ranks stepped a member of the orchestra to join the action as a crusty old man wishing to rid himself of his wife!

In 1984, Bob Bickle produced *The Government Inspector* and, in 1987, *The Heiress*. The former engaged the interest of the press, in that the Inspector and his wife were played by a newly-wedded young couple in the village. A straight play, this required a large cast of 24 which offered scope for a great many people to enjoy amateur acting.

Irene Wright's production *Outside Edge* was of particular interest to the cricketing fraternity in the village but although well supported by those who like to wear the white flannels, this lively comedy was also enjoyed by those with no sporting pretensions whatever.

A different event was Leslie Read's poetry evening that took place in the Village Orchard, an idyllic setting where the weather matched the charm of the programme of verse. Then, 'Apple Day', in 1992, masterminded by Erica, was an imaginative project where the theme of apples was reflected in food and drink served through the day, music and poetry to underline the delights of orchards and the fruit they bear, and baskets of different varieties of English apples with their country names (*see Chapter 3, pp73–76*).

During the 1990s, the two straight plays were *She Stoops To Conquer* and *Roses of Eyam*. The latter, in rehearsal, was not universally welcomed, as word got out that it was about the Derbyshire village struck down by plague in 1665/66 and where was the fun in that? Not too much, it has to be said, but when the curtain rose on a street scene in Eyam, marvellously realised by the scene painter, Barbara Jaggs, and when the gripping story of a village, not dissimilar to our own, unfolded, all was forgiven. Once again, Will Carnell composed music, both evocative and appealing.

The millennium was celebrated by the village as a whole in June 2000, the brainchild of resident Don Badger, who asked the Drama Group for an appropriate offering to mark the day. A new member of the group, John King, organised a group of young people to present *The Millennium in Fifteen Minutes*, which they performed twice in the Orchard. This was followed by the 'Shakespeare Players', alias Lustleigh Drama Group, wheeling an antique wagon filled with props across the Green, to rehearse scenes from *A Midsummer Night's Dream* under the apple trees. The Director felt it providential that the second showing was the last, as lunch in 'Ye Cleavage Ale House' between times had made for a more lively rendering of the piece than expected – and the wheel of the cart fell off!

The year 2001 saw its own sad drama when the foot and mouth epidemic hit Devon. And this in the year when, before the epidemic took hold, the group had decided upon *Cold Comfort Farm* as a May production and rehearsals were well on the way. Irony indeed! Hoping for the best outcome for our local farmers, rehearsals continued. Luck held, and one of the first village events as the epidemic waned, was the presentation of this play, to full houses for three nights. It was almost as though a sigh of relief went up from players and village alike.

One could not write about drama in Lustleigh without touching upon the joy of pantomime. There have been many over the years – *Dick Whittington* twice, *Cinderella, Mother Goose, Aladdin, The Wizard of Oz*. Villagers, who seldom offer to tread the boards on other occasions, will often emerge for a part in a pantomime. Pantomime dames, principal boys, rats, cats, genies, princesses with long tresses, wicked

Mother Goose, *February 1995, with Dave Wills and daughter Emma.*

Leigh Wakeham as Constance and Sheila Schroeder as the maid in She Stoops to Conquer.

witches, fairy queens – all have graced the stage and delighted audiences over the years. Unoriginal last-night japes, despair of directors and instant joy to the perpetrators never fail to lace the Saturday-night brew – plaits pinned to the scenery, lipstick kisses planted on Buttons, the sudden appearance of hitherto unknown and unwanted props. Messrs Dave Wills and Len Harvey perfected a study of these during their halcyon panto days. And who could forget the transformation scene in Erica Read's *Cinderella*, a truly memorable magical moment, achieved by a dedicated stage crew and Erica's persistence and expertise.

Another activity that the village takes to heart is the Old Time Music Hall such as John King produced in December 2000. An eventful day of floods that cut off the village and deprived the singers of their pianist also forced the cancellation of the first night. However, the next two nights were uproarious and convivial enough to cheer all dampened spirits!

A glance through past minute-books shows up a few constants. In 1977 there was a plea for willing producers, who 'seem to be few and far between'. Also in short supply, then as now, men to take the many roles written for them. In 1979 'it was difficult to cast due to a shortage of men.' Present-day producers would reply 'Tell me about it!' Then, of course, in 1980, 'subscriptions were very slow coming in'!

But, over and above it all, the word 'enjoy' shines through like a beacon. Past programmes list the names of actors, stage crew, lighting and sound technicians, make-up ladies, front of house, which read like a village roll call. We participate in this activity for the enjoyment of audience and actors alike, and when that participation is in the good company of friends, as it is in Lustleigh, we have a tradition to uphold and something to cherish.

Saturday Morning Junior Drama Club

This group, set up by this contributor in 1982, comprised young people from the ages of eight to fifteen. They met in Church House, an ideal space for this Saturday morning club, which named itself the Junior Drama Club. This was a very happy and successful activity that ran for five years. There was a particularly village flavour to these Saturday mornings when the rule was that anyone arriving after the church clock finished striking nine was deemed late – and every Saturday saw the virtuous standing outside the door on the verandah, counting with the striking of the clock as young last-minute actors came tearing across the Green, trying to climb the steps before the final knell!

The first play was the *Somerset Mummers' Play*, performed at Christmas in the Village Hall, in a double bill along with children from Bovey Tracey Primary School who presented 'A Dancing Song for Christmas'. Both groups processed across the Green after meeting up in Church House, a sight wonderfully heart-warming and appropriate to the season and to their effort for the charity Shelter, to which they contributed the proceeds.

Three full-length plays followed, and Will Carnell composed songs and incidental music that were such a contribution to the success of each. The first was an adaptation of Roald Dahl's *James and the Giant Peach*. Then came *The Golden Goose* with three naughty sisters, a clever young fellow seeking his fortune and a golden-haired princess. The final *Bunches of Roses* was the work of a pretty mature group of young players whose improvisation and imagination were incorporated into the adaptation of a story by the children's writer Joan Aitken.

Other smaller-scale activities occurred during these years – more presentations at charity coffee mornings, and an afternoon with 'Worzel Gummidge' ending with tea in the garden at Well Park.

Along with the many photographs are the many memories. There was the evening when the large audience of well-wishing relations was assembled, the children on the stage behind the curtains in a state of nervous excitement – and no pianist. Unaware of a rather early time for curtain up, he did a heroic sprint when summoned and his late arrival was relayed to those on stage by the grave announcement: 'The orchestra has arrived'. And the play went on. On another occasion the prompt book went missing and a member of the audience was found quietly reading it, as it was a favourite story from her youth!

This group remained much the same for five years – steadily growing older until it was time to move on. It is a time to look back upon with great affection.

LUSTLEIGH CRICKET CLUB

A brief history, culled from the Parish Magazine, *the 50th Anniversary Programme of 1988 (kindly lent by Richard Hughes) and brought up to date by Barry Goff.*

The first mention of cricket in the *Parish Magazine* occurs in the very first issue, namely August 1888, where the newly-appointed rector, the Reverend Henry Tudor (who was also the editor) wrote as follows:

The Lustleigh Cricket Team, which is this year under the management of Mr Carew-Hunt meets on most evenings of the week for practice, in a field adjoining the Cleave Hotel. The first match of the season was to have been played on Wednesday 25th July v the East Ogwell Eleven, but owing to the rain which fell heavily all that day, had to be postponed. The choir boys play cricket every Saturday in one of the fields at the rectory. We hope that there will be a good attendance of these boys during the rest of the season.

And from the September 1888 issue:

The Lustleigh Team, with Mr Lionel Gould as Captain, have been working fairly hard during the past month, practice has been kept up regularly nearly every evening, and up to the 24 inst three matches have been played;

1. *Lustleigh v Ashburton, played at Lustleigh, resulting in a victory for the former.*
2. *Lustleigh v Bovey, played at Bovey in which the Bovey team was victorious.*
3. *Lustleigh v Chudleigh, played at Lustleigh. Lustleigh won easily by six wickets.*

In October 1888 there was an analysis of the successful season in which Lustleigh won eight and lost only one match. The top batting averages were achieved by C.P. Wills whose average score was 20 runs over 10 innings, and L.F. Gould who averaged 15 runs over 15 innings.

Lustleigh Cricket Club as we know it today was founded in 1938 and there is little information about cricket happenings in the years between 1888 and 1938. In 1988 the club celebrated a 'Glorious Half Century' with the publication of a 50th Anniversary Programme containing a comprehensive history of 50 years of cricketing progress. Cricket before 1938 is dismissed rather briefly (which would have upset Henry Tudor):

Lustleigh has always been keener on cricket than football, but there was a team in the 1920s, c.1925.
Left to right, back row: *W. Major, J. Netley, A. Horrell, ? Gribble, Mark Germon;* front includes: *E. Bunclarke, M. Morecombe and W. (Bill) Waldron. Photograph supplied by Douglas Germon, son of Mark.*

The early history of cricket in Lustleigh is lost in the mists of time, but the game was played on some kind of regular basis from the end of the First World War. In those days the team was part of the Lustleigh Sports Club.

But the progress and successes of the club in the post-war years are faithfully documented, although it is possible here only to reprint some highlights from the 50-year record of village cricket.

The cricket field and the pavilion were constantly at the forefront of the club's concerns:

Two alternative venues were considered in 1938. The first was the Sports Field and the second Mr S. Amery's field. The latter was originally decided upon although, as already mentioned, the Committee minutes for 1938 show that the Sports (now Cricket) field was finally chosen.

A notice to quit was received in 1957 and reported to the AGM, whereupon we read:

One gets the impression that the Club was harnessing all its available power and was moving into action… Mrs Egerton (the owner of the field) was persuaded to let the Club use the field again in 1958, and a change of ownership enabled the 1959 AGM to hear, surely with a sigh of relief, that agreement had been reached with the new owner for the Club to continue to use the field.

The programme makes note of notorious players and performances:

The original enthusiasm of 1938 which produced 54 names and expressions of interest has persisted, although the number of playing members, not surprisingly for a community as small as Lustleigh, has sometimes dwindled to the point where the Club could barely honour its commitments.

It determined to carry on, however:

… and carry on it did, only to hear – at the 1956 AGM – the Chairman, Dr S. Daly, once again drawing members' attention to the very serious shortage of players, only seven being available for the season. This, together with the 'poor and dangerous' condition of the pitch, made the 1956 season doubtful. Once more, however, the membership prevailed, and after Mr K.C. Fry, Mr W.F. Horrell and Mr P. Woolley had spoken on the subject (heartening stuff) the meeting unanimously declared its intention of continuing.

But the problem would not go away and by 1970 it had again become a crucial issue: 'The committee was informed by the Captain, Len Harvey, that the number of potential players had dropped by five since the previous season.' Advertising was resorted

The Colts Cricket Team in front of a house along Wreyland Path, 1948. Left to right, standing: *Chris Cadle, Bill Saunders, J.W.C. Collier (headmaster of Lustleigh School), Lionel Morecombe, John Gould, Douglas Germon, Richard Sanders;* sitting: *Mervyn Hatherley, Bill Wills, Leonard Wright, Bill Sneep, Bob Gilbertson.*

Water Washout!

Above and right: *Floods on the cricket field, 1960.*

Below: *More floods, November 1980.*

to and the situation was saved: 'Needless to say. The AGM would not countenance the abandonment of the Club, and it moved from strength to strength to the present day.'

The programme also contained the following note:

Centuries have been rare on the Lustleigh ground, in spite of the fairly short boundaries, and only four have been scored by Lustleigh players, as follows:

1952	*J.W.C. Collier*	*100*
1961	*Courtney Wright*	*106*
1973	*Barry Widdicombe*	*120*
1985	*Steve Germon*	*109*

There have, of course, been times of despondency, such as the two rather sound defeats of June 1960 – all out for 11 against Ashton, and all out for 14 against Bovey Tracey! However, low scores like these seem to be a thing of the past, and it seems safe to say that the team, like the Club in general, is thriving.

Team captains are all enumerated in the Jubilee programme. There are too many names to record in this short review but some individual captaincies stand out: Douglas Germon for ten years from 1959; the Wright family variously for 1973, 1977–79, 1981–84 and 1987–88; and Len Harvey for 1969–72.

So ends this brief and sadly rather perfunctory review of Lustleigh cricket over the 100 years from 1888 to 1988. Barry Goff takes the story onwards.

Since 1988 the Cricket Club has gone from strength to strength. At that time it enjoyed a rich 20th-century history of being a most hospitable club with banter and leg-pulling as much a part of the day's cricket as winning or losing. The environment and standard of the wicket was the envy of most clubs. By 1993 we entered, for the first time, the Brockman K.O. Cup, intended for village clubs in the South Devon area. In this first year we reached the final, played at Torquay, and narrowly lost to Brixham. In subsequent years we have raised the level of our ability and competitiveness to such a degree that we reached the final again in 1996, but were well beaten by a very good Paignton eleven. In 1996 we defeated Dartington to lift the trophy for the first time and to date we have not lost a single game in this competition, winning in 1997, '98, '99, 2000 and 2001. Many local observers would now like to see us no more in this competition.

In 1994 we entered the South Devon Cricket League and finished fourth despite needing to clinch only one more game to win it! In 1996 we won the League with an unbeaten record. In this year we also opened our new Club house situated in its present elevated position. This further enhanced our facilities and afforded an infinitely improved viewing position. We have since added mains water and electricity and installed a septic tank to accommodate the showers and toilets – with money all raised by local effort.

We have retained the title of Partnership Publishing South Devon Cricket League A Division winners in every year since 1996, and with an unblemished seven out of seven in 2001 are well on track to retain this title for a sixth year running. All in all a most healthy state of affairs for a village club with a village outlook and a committed group of hard working players and officials.

The Cricket Pavilion, since replaced.

The cricketing Wright family. Left to right: *Mike, Courtenay, Shaun and Steve.*

Lustleigh Cricket Club, c.1978.

THE PARISH MAGAZINE

by Joe Crowdy (Parish Magazine Editor)

Lustleigh's *Parish Magazine* first appeared in August 1888, founded by the newly-installed rector, the Reverend Henry Tudor (the son-in-law of his predecessor, the Reverend Frederic Ensor, rector from 1847 to 1887). Only a month before he started the magazine the new rector had been inducted into the living when, on 12 July 1888, it is recorded that the Archdeacon of Totnes gave a 'practical, useful address'. The item continues: 'The service was that in use in this diocese, and helps to bring before people and pastor the deep responsibility of the office and work of Parish Priest.'

Judging by his writings in the early years of the magazine, Henry Tudor was imbued with a deep sense of social conscience towards his small flock of some 400 souls. His opening editorial reflects the pattern of his concern:

> *There are now very many parishes in England, some of them with smaller populations than Lustleigh, in which there is a Parish Magazine and we hope the* Lustleigh Magazine *may help to record parish history and give information and notices of coming events, which may be of interest to those who read it.*

There is no doubt that, during his 15 years of ministry, this well-loved rector displayed his commitment and paternalism in all matters both spiritual and temporal which affected the life of the parish. Some of the excerpts reproduced below demonstrate not only the breadth and depth of his wide-ranging interests but also illustrate, by way of his many percipient comments, something of the flavour of village life at the end of the 19th century. Here was a rector and editor who was truly father to his parishioners, striving to improve the conditions for all and, in particular, to alleviate the hardships of the poor; and it should be remembered that poverty in the last decade of the century was a real and ugly entity. Even in a rural parish such as Lustleigh – where most cottagers kept a pig and grew their own vegetables – it remained a continuing struggle to raise a family (and many families were often large) on the standard agricultural wage of 10 shillings a week.

The extracts begin more than 100 years ago:

June 1890
The Church will be left open on Week-days from 10.15am to 5pm until further notice. It is hoped that those who enter it will remember that it is God's House of Prayer, and that they will behave reverently and preserve it from injury, and if unfortunately any person do any damage to the Church, that notice be given at once to Mr S Nicholls, Sexton, who lives opposite the East End of the Church. Next door to the policeman.

January 1891
The present winter is said by many in this neighbourhood to be one of the most severe which they can remember, especially coming as snow has this year, before Christmas. We are pleased to say that through some kind help, and the offertory, it has been possible this year to give to over forty persons, two pounds of beef, and two cwt. of coal or two shilling worth of grocery. It may not be possible to do so much another year, but we are glad that in severe weather so much has been done in addition to other gifts which parishioners have given personally.

July 1891
The Census. The population of Lustleigh in 1881 was 366, and is now believed to be in 1891... 404.

October 1892
We congratulate Mr Squires, Waywarden, on the improvement which he has carried out on the road near the Old Vestry, and on the repairs being effected on Mapstone Hill. Lustleigh roads need improvement and are difficult to manage... The drainage works will soon be finished.

February 1893
As there are two cases of Scarlet Fever at Brookfield, it is earnestly to be hoped that all persons will use the gift of common sense with which God has endowed them, and do all in their power to prevent this terrible disease from spreading.

March 1894
Complaints, we are sorry to hear, are made that a few foolish boys and girls collect sometimes outside the railway station, and annoy persons by their bad behaviour and bad language. We hope this foolish conduct will cease. It would be a disgrace if anyone was summoned before the magistrates for bad conduct.

October 1895
October is a good month to plant creepers. If this was more generally done ugly houses might become pleasant looking. Any offerings of suitable ivy or creepers or roses for the Churchyard wall will be thankfully received by the Rector.

October 1896
We hope some of our readers will not mind our once more saying, that many a house in Lustleigh would look prettier and more homely if roses, ivies or creepers were planted to run over the walls. It is not too late in the year to do this at once, the holes into which the roots are put should be deep and filled with good earth.

January 1897
Everybody will be glad to hear that Mary Ann Coles seems likely to recover. After she had been a short time at Teignmouth the Typhoid fever attacked her and her

life was in very great danger. She has been admirably nursed and cared for in Teignmouth Hospital, and if she recovers or not a very great debt of gratitude will be due. A case of typhoid fever in a hospital like Teignmouth, which is not meant for infectious cases, has caused much trouble and expense, and various people have suggested that Lustleigh should do something for that Hospital. Mrs Wise, Miss Morris and HT have promised ten shillings each, and any donations, small or great, will be thankfully received by Miss Tudor.

We stated in our last Magazine that the cost of the Clothing Club was £4.7s. for this year, the Offertory on a recent Sunday was £1.7s., any donation to lessen the deficit, will be thankfully received.

December 1898
The Revd G Y Comyns preached an interesting Sermon on Temperance, on Sunday last, we hope some good effect will follow from it, by God's blessing.

Sadly there are no copies of the *Parish Magazine* available for the closing years of Henry Tudor's reign as rector and editor. His successor, the Reverend William Gordon Baillie took over in 1904 but neither he nor subsequent rectors and editors displayed the same flair for paternalistic benevolence that characterised Henry Tudor's monthly writings. He was the father of the village and occupied a pre-eminent position which no one sought to question. When the Parish Council was created in 1894 he automatically became the Chairman, rightly dispensing with any suggestions that Council Chairmen should be democratically elected.

In the 100 years that followed Henry Tudor's editorship, the magazine has had its ups and downs; sadly rather more of the latter than the former. Until the middle of the last century the local news appeared as a pale shadow wrapped round the sometimes rather saccharine pages of the *Church Monthly*. But latterly, lay editors have taken over and two pioneering individuals – Lt Cdr Wallace Kemp and his successor, Betty Raikes – rescued the magazine from its lethargy as an addendum to the *Diocesan News*. Today – the editor likes to think – the *Lustleigh Parish Magazine* is sturdily independent

representing not only the Church (under whose generous patronage it continues to be published – and indeed the opening editorial is always the 'Rector's Letter'), but the wider interests of the whole village, thus fulfilling the precepts set out by Henry Tudor in 1888: 'to record parish history and to give information and notices of coming events, which may be of interest to those who read it.'

Lustleigh Parish Magazine, 2001.

LUSTLEIGH MAY DAY
by Belinda Baudouy

The May Day Festival dates back to the Roman Festival of Flora, the Goddess of Flowers. It has possibly been traditional in England since Roman times. It was customary during the Middle Ages for everyone to go out 'a-maying' at an early hour, to collect fresh flowers with which to crown the fairest maid of the village, the Queen of the May.

Lustleigh almost certainly held its own ceremony but this had lapsed until it was revived in its present form at the beginning of the 20th century by Mr Cecil Torr, who, in his own inimitable style, writes of it thus:

There is a May-day festival here, for which I am responsible. There used to be dancing around the May-pole at the flower-show and other festivals, but none upon May-day itself: and I put an end to that anomaly.

The crowning took place on the hillside above Wreyland, off Willmead Lane, where the names of the May Queens are carved on a granite boulder. In 1954 the ceremony was moved to a new site and the May Queen's throne was set up on a rock in the Orchard, where all subsequent names have been recorded.

This celebration of May Day takes place in Lustleigh on the first Saturday in May each year beginning in the early afternoon at the entrance to the Town Orchard. A magnificent canopy of flowers, which has been prepared that morning by ladies of the village, is carried over the May Queen by her four canopy bearers as she leads the procession of maypole dancers around the village. Her crown of fresh flowers and white lily (grown locally) are carried alongside. The procession stops at the church steps where she is blessed by the rector and the children sing songs. Everyone then returns to the Orchard where the queen is crowned on the May Day Rock. The Maypole dancing then begins.

During the afternoon, teas are served in the Village Hall. A brass band plays and Morris Dancers perform in the Orchard where many other entertainments are enjoyed.

Lustleigh May Queens

1905	Mabel Bunclarke	1934	Nellie Wills	1973	Diane Aggett
1906	Olive Chudley	1935	Barbara Weeks	1974	Caroline Williams
1907	Annie Menhennett	1936	Veronica Yeoman	1975	Annette Stephens
1908	Amy Wyatt	1937	Eileen Dray	1976	Catherine Beaumont
1909	Florrie Valance	1938	Phyllis Wills	1977	Debbie Seabrook
1910	Ethel Squires	1939	Edna Dray	1978	Heather Wright
1911	Alice Howard	1940	Rosie Olding	1979	Julie Osborne
1912	Dorothy Motton			1980	Susan Aggett
1913	Muriel Brimblecombe			1981	Rebecca French
1914	Janie Lake	**1941–53 no ceremonies**		1982	Jeanette Palmer
1915	Guinevere Morecombe			1983	Lisa Rowe
1916	Irene Crockford	1954	Gillian Williams	1984	Debbie Goodfellow
1917	May Yeoman	1955	Myra Brock	1985	Sarah Jane Lilley
1918	Gertrude Parker	1956	Patricia Powell	1986	Carolyn Tapson
1919	Gladys Waldron	1957	Janet Horrell	1987	Sally Ann Lilley
1920	Vera Hill	1958	Helen Beard	1988	Rebecca Merriott
1921	May Wonnacott	1959	Christine Moore	1989	Kim Hopwood
1922	Phyllis Yeoman	1960	Iona Jones	1990	Coralie Olver
1923	Florrie Aggett	1961	Jayne Nelson	1991	Abigail Mabey
1924	Josephine Wilson	1962	Jennifer Perry	1992	Katie Jacoby
1925	Romola Wills	1963	Ruth Matthews	1993	Simone Olver
1926	Dolly White	1964	Carola Woodger	1994	Lisa Roberts
1927	Phyllis Wills	1965	Jaqueline Kennett	1995	Natalie Davis
1928	Kathleen Cooper	1966	Patricia Johnson	1996	Rebecca Drewett
1929	Mary Marshall	1967	Angela Woodger	1997	Laura Dale
1930	Winifred Horrell	1968	Vivienne Jenkin	1998	Louise Baudouy
1931	Brenda Osborne	1969	Suzanne Beaumont	1999	Daisy Beare
1932	May Clarke	1970	Jane Aggett	2000	Emma Wills
1933	Winifred Olding	1971	Wendy Harvey	2001	Joely Badger
		1972	Julie Germon		

Procession of May Queen Winifred Olding along Knowle Road towards Brookside, 1933.

Lustleigh May Day

The May Queen of 1906, Olive Chudley.

May Day, 1933, May Queen Winifred Olding on the church steps.

Lustleigh May Day

Left: *May Day being celebrated on the old site, date unknown.*

Below: *May Day, 2000.*

Above and inset: *Simone Olver, 1993 May Queen, on her throne in the Orchard.*

121

THE LUSTLEIGH SOCIETY
by Joe Crowdy (Chairman)

It is appropriate that the Lustleigh Society, which by its energy and initiative has sponsored this book, should merit a few lines to tell of its history and function. Its purpose is best defined by reference to the constitution which states that its objects are:

1. To study and promote an interest in the history, archaeology and natural history of Lustleigh and its environs.
2. To promote an interest and care for the buildings, monuments and other objects of historic or general interest in Lustleigh and its neighbourhood.
3. To provide a repository for any documents, papers, photographs and other items relative to [1] and [2] above.
4. To help preserve the character and traditions of Lustleigh and its environs.

It has to be said that the Society is better at preserving historical documents and other evidence of Lustleigh's past history than it is at caring for its own documentation; details of its origins are incomplete and hard to come by but there seems little doubt that the Society was formed in June 1978 when the late Lieutenant Commander Wallace Kemp was the first Chairman and the late Reverend Doctor Frederic Mason the first honorary Secretary. Some time later Wallace Kemp became the first President and Dr Mason the Chairman.

At present (2001) the Society numbers some 75 members and conducts an enterprising programme of monthly lecture presentations during the winter months and visits to sites of archaeological, historical and ecological interest during the summer months.

The jewel in the Society's crown is the Archives Room in the Old Vestry (the building in the churchyard which was originally the village school founded by Parson Davy in 1825) where have been collected an impressive assembly of village documents, pictures and maps (including the 1837 Tithe Map of the village).

As far back as 1998 the Society perceived the need for a history of Lustleigh but the enterprise made no real progress until member Tim Hall linked the proposal to the practical sponsorship of the present publishers (Halsgrove of Tiverton) and thereafter the concept made real strides forward only to face cancellation in 1999 when Tim found he could no longer manage the commitment. There being no rush of volunteers to take on the task, it fell by default to the present writer who hopes that you – the reader – will find the final product a worthy endeavour.

LUSTLEIGH HORTICULTURAL SOCIETY
by Margaret Bowen

The first recorded official notice of our society was in the first volume of the first edition of the *Parish Magazine* issued in August 1888. It even then referred to the first show as being held the previous year (1887) when, interestingly, it was held in conjunction with the Lustleigh branch of the 'Rational Sick and Burial Society'! It had obviously been up and thriving for some considerable time under the name of The Horticultural and Cottage Garden Society, and while the Cottage Garden Society held an annual competition – the gardens were inspected three times a year and then judged – the Flower Show was only then inaugurated. There is a reference to the fact that 'many fine plants were kindly lent for decoration by the resident gentry, so that the tent presented quite a gay appearance.' This presumably was because the majority of growers concentrated on vegetables and fruit; in fact, over 2000 potatoes (of all shapes and sizes) were on display which rather bears out this premise. Even at this very first show, it was not kept exclusively for garden matters as knitting and needlework were included and also prizes were given for butter and honey, all in a roundly representative array.

Although the show grew in size, broadened its appeal and became more embracing with pony events, athletic sports, classes for farm horses, craft stalls and animal displays, etc., the whole thing was still run and organised by the Horticultural Society. (In fact, the Society ran the whole Lustleigh Show until 1991.)

Oft quoted and frequently referred to is the exceedingly graphic and highly entertaining report of the 1900 show in Cecil Torr's *Small Talk at Wreyland* in which his friend narrated the spectacle of utter chaos that enveloped the show that year:

We went in about 2, when it opened, and found some disorder in the main tent, as it had partially blown down early. Then there was a horrible noise, and a great gust of wind ripped the poultry tent almost in half. The whole thing began to collapse, men were rushing in and being pulled out by screaming females, some were tightening the ropes, which others immediately loosened, and presently a great loose flap of canvas overturned the stand of cages – a horrid mass of ducks and fowls screaming and quacking and flapping all over the crowd, pursued by their owners and upsetting everything. And, just at this moment the big flower marquee – which was of course deserted – was caught by a tremendous puff of wind and torn right up and dropped on the tables inside. It wasn't heavy enough to be dangerous, but I wish I could give you any idea of how funny it was to see (a well known character) creep from under the canvas with an old lady, an infuriated fowl pecking at his knickerbockered calves. One of the nicest incidents was a little old lady in a velvet mantle and black curls, careering backwards over the ground, knocking people over as she clutched at the tail of a huge escaping and crowing cock with one hand, and with the other arm embraced a captured but still struggling and squawking goose. In about an hour after it was opened everything on the ground was swept quite flat. But excursion trains kept arriving, whose innocent passengers paid their sixpences – you couldn't see the ruin from outside – and wondered why the crowd assembled at the gate laughed at them. However, it was worth while to see the village boys fighting and scrambling under the fallen tent for the apples and potatoes.

The society continued with ups and downs – there being frequent reminders in the old *Parish Magazines* to 'please pay subscriptions' (a cri de coeur and still a perennial problem). With short stoppages during the 1914–18 and 1939–45 wars, it was re-inaugurated in 1946 when it was agreed that the annual subscriptions would be 2s.6d. but that those desirous of becoming Vice Presidents, should contribute 10s.6d. per annum. In many of the minutes that followed there were always promises to become affiliated to the Royal Horticultural Society 'if and when funds become available'.

The Cottage Garden competition was revived for a short time in a different format but, alas, lack of sufficient interest caused its demise. In 1987/88 a specialist rose and delphinium show was created but the broader appeal of the annual show was felt to be more embracing and the enthusiasm for this also waned.

Since 1974 it had been suggested that perhaps the burden of organising the whole of the annual show could be shared. This topic was frequently discussed and debated but only in 1990 was a new committee formed to run the Lustleigh Show. This enabled the Horticultural Society to concentrate on its own event which had been steadily growing and the entries multiplying. Henceforth it would take place as before but under the banner of the Lustleigh Show. The first show under the new management was held in 1991 and thereafter the Horticultural Society was able to devote its zeal to the running of its spring and summer exhibitions.

Of course, the energies of the society are not entirely devoted to the shows – there are extensive and fascinating visits to gardens of note and interest. And now, moreover, the society is affiliated to the RHS, and an annual trip to Rosemoor is one of the great treats. Guest gardeners and lecturers are invited who are a fund of information and on top of their subjects; on the whole they spur members on to greater things but occasionally they have a

The Spring Flower Show in 2000 in the Village Hall.

discouraging effect as it seems impossible to be able to achieve such exquisite perfection. Nevertheless, they allow the society – during the long winter months when those talks are generally given – to fantasise about their summer borders and enormous future blooms.

In 1985 under the Chairmanship of Frank Evans, the society hosted the BBC's prestigious 'Gardeners' Question Time'. This was a great coup and a huge success. Again, in 2000 – with Ann Harvey as Chairman – another two editions of the programme were broadcast from the Village Hall. These were made together but transmitted over the airwaves on different weeks – as if from different locations. It was rather like a secret in which we willingly participated! A large assortment of questions was put to the panel, from invasive bamboo to non-maturing figs and, of course, the dreaded slug managed to raise its ugly head!

The society has many charms and is joined for a variety of reasons. Without doubt, the showing of specimens is one of the principal attractions – many a tale of skulduggery and sharp practice is told. One exhibitor named William Cole (and the tales about

this character are legend and much repeated) even took to pricking his beans with a pin under the calyx in order to identify them as he was convinced that his exhibit had been stolen and staged under someone else's name! This way he could confront the culprit! And this was in very recent times; no doubt in days of yore more vengeance was meted out, although there is, perhaps fortunately, no record of Horticultural Society members resorting to violence.

Today, the society thrives although 'please pay subscriptions' remains an annual plea. The membership numbers are healthy, although they fluctuate, and the interest in gardens and gardening never palls.

Right: *A Lustleigh garden in bloom.*

Below: *BBC 'Gardeners' Question Time' in the Village Hall filled to capacity, 25 April 2000.*

LUSTLEIGH SHOW
by Bill Jackson

The Lustleigh Show, held on the August bank holiday Monday, is the largest annual event to be held in the village. Over the years the show has evolved from a modest gymkhana and horticultural exhibition to one that now attracts over 3000 visitors (who arrive in about 800 cars!).

It is not known when the show started or how the format was developed through the years but we know that the show activities were suspended during the Second World War and from the minutes of the inaugural meeting held on 19 November 1946 we are told of the proceedings of Lustleigh Horticultural Society's first meeting after the war. The committee consisted of the following members, many of whose names may sound familiar to local readers: Captain N.L. Cooper (Chairman), Colonel J. Raikes (Vice Chairman), Major Bloomer (Hon. Secretary), Mr Thackwell Lewis (Treasurer). Other members were: Captain Coverton, Colonel Fawcett, Mrs M.M. Burton, Mr Wiggins, Mr P. Bunclarke, Mr J. Knight, Mr Richard Bourne, Mr Philps, Mr S. Amery, Mr Germon, Mr Horrell and Mrs Reid.

Many interesting facts emerge from this meeting including a proposal that the trustees of the old Lustleigh Agricultural & Horticultural Society should be asked to transfer any funds in their possession to the new society. The annual flower show was planned to be held on August bank holiday Monday in the Conservative Hall (now the Village Hall) but at a meeting held on 20 February 1947 it was decided that the hall would not be at all suitable and Mr Amery 'kindly placed a very excellently placed field, just off the main Bovey Tracey road, at the disposal of the society for the flower show.' The subsequent meetings saw the rules and conditions being formulated and great debates on marquee and tent hire and insurance. Entry charges were set at 2s.0d. per person, children were admitted half price and cars were 2s.6d. to include the driver only. There was concern about the liability for entertainment tax and the Treasurer was asked to investigate.

During the next few years the show became a major local attraction including one of the most important goat shows in the region attracting entries from all over the South West. A gymkhana and a dog show were added and all was organised by the main Horticultural Society committee. A dance was also arranged in the evening after the show in the Conservative Hall with a dance band being hired and refreshments laid on.

In the 1950s the show continued to grow with a larger horse show and gymkhana and the event generally became more adventurous. Water was laid on courtesy of the Johnson family (and still is to the current day!), electricity by generator was organised

in later years, but there was no mention of any formal toilet arrangements until many years later!

The horse show had its own sub-committee as the attraction grew larger, the secretary having an office consisting of a 12' x 12' tent. There were, as with most events of this kind, many amusing situations occurring, although in general not funny at the time for those involved. One such incident happened in 1962 when a grey pony with rider careered into the secretary's tent, knocking over tables, and scattering money and result forms in all directions. Pony, still with rider on board, then left with everyone unscathed but well shaken up. Fortunately the customary crate of beer and bottle of whisky in the tent escaped damage in the mayhem.

Two interesting letters from the archives, following the death of King George VI in 1952, are reproduced below; they reflect the degree of respect and formality customary 50 years ago:

*From the President of the
Lustleigh Horticultural Society,
Rear Admiral [S] E H Drayson [ret] CB, CBE*

*To Her Majesty the Queen Mother,
Buckingham Palace. SW1*

9th February 1952

Your Majesty,

We, who are members of the Lustleigh Horticultural Society and the devoted and loyal subjects of His late Majesty and His Gracious Queen pray Your Majesty and Your Royal Family, to accept our most deep and sincere sympathy at the passing of a great King who never failed to inspire us with resolution when our country was in danger and whose selfless devotion to His most exacting duty has been so great an encouragement to us in our daily tasks.

I have the honour to be Your Majesty's most obedient humble servant,

signed E H Drayson

The Queen Mother's Lady-in-Waiting, on Buckingham Palace notepaper formally bordered in deepest black, replied as follows:

March 11th, 1952

Dear Admiral Drayson, I am commanded by Queen Elizabeth, The Queen Mother, to thank you and all those for whom you speak for your most kind message. The thoughts and sympathy which surround her have greatly strengthened Her Majesty.

The show expanded gradually with the addition of sideshows to entertain members of the family and friends who may not enjoy the same enthusiasm for horses or horticulture. These included many traditional activities and games such as hoopla, skittles, the greasy pole, tossing the sheaf, lawnmower racing, tug of war, catapults, giant football, bottle stall, and many others.

During the ensuing decades the show flourished and became increasingly popular with new ideas being added but always maintaining the traditional core attractions of the horticultural exhibition with gymkhana.

In 1990 the Horticultural Society was finding it increasingly difficult to run the large village show and organise the horticulture exhibition and consequently a completely new committee was established whose main objective was to manage the show for both the Horticultural Society and gymkhana. Since that time the show has grown significantly and although attractions vary from year to year, they have included: the 10km run; a carriage drive through six local farms; a dog show and terrier racing; an archery competition; a display of owls; a donkey sanctuary display; the pets and small animals show; the Kelly Mine display; static working engines; a parachute display; swings and roundabout; Punch and Judy; the Rural Skills Trust; a sheep-shearing demonstration and competition; wood cutting and axe demonstration; and Fire Brigade demonstrations.

In the more recent shows a jazz band has played outside the beer and wine tent. There has also been a good choice of food and drink to cater for the numbers attending and the increasingly more demanding expectations of our visitors. There are typically 40 trade stands (with minimum duplication of produce!) and about 10 craft stalls offering interesting articles and demonstrating clever skills.

In the mid 1990s a further committee was established to run the Saturday evening dance and cabaret. The initial idea was to make more use of the expensive marquee that was erected on Friday but was not previously utilised until the Monday. This committee has done a fine job of putting on first-class entertainment and food for some 400 people.

The show has had its setbacks; 25 April 1997 was a bad day. The barn containing all the show assets was destroyed by fire and would cost some £3000 and many man-hours to replace. To indicate the scale of the disaster, the committee lost all of the games including an ancient hoopla table, 400 fence posts, 2000 yards of rope, 15 horse jumps, 400 yards of alkathene water pipe, stand pipes and fittings, and all the show signs. Many committee members worked extremely hard over the next few weeks and amazingly the August show went ahead as usual. Due to sound financial policies set up by the committee, whereby funds are retained to provide for up to two washout shows, the replacements needed could be purchased without delay.

In 1998 the horse show was set up as an autonomous committee with separate accounting facilities. The show organisation now consists of the main committee working with three associate committees, namely the Horticultural Society, the Horse Show Committee and the Dance Committee.

The Horticultural Society put on a splendid exhibition with over 130 classes mainly of course for vegetables and flowers but also with classes for floral art, cookery, photography, handicrafts and preserves. The Horse Show Committee runs a very popular event with typically 18 classes in three rings, mostly competitive and varied classes but some just for fun mainly for the younger children.

In 2001 there was, sadly, a smaller show due to the risks associated with foot and mouth disease. The field available was much smaller and there was regrettably no horse show and no trade stands, although the Horticultural Show was as successful as usual together with all the now customary catering arrangements, side shows, and demonstrations; the evening dance was run as planned.

Over recent years the show has generated a cash surplus and this has been distributed to village causes such as the Village Hall, playground equipment and the Cricket Club pavilion funds. We have always been very fortunate to be able to hold the show on the best site in Lustleigh considering the road access, good visual impact and relatively flat fields. We are most grateful to Kelly Farm for this facility.

It is impossible to conclude this account of our Show without mention of that always unpredictable factor and popular topic of conversation – the weather. For more than ten years the weather on Show Day has been quite remarkably good or, indeed, very good, thus defying our characteristically pessimistic outlook on our English climate. To find a show that was seriously affected we have to go back to 1986 when on Monday 26 August – Show day – 62.7mm (nearly 3 inches) of rain fell between 9a.m. and 9p.m. The result was a dreadful washout and nearly all the field activities had to be cancelled. The water gathered in the gateways over 12 inches deep and wellington boots gave little help because the current was flowing so quickly. Land Rovers ferried the less prepared back to their cars but the problems did not stop there because the water had made the fields impassable to the average car and therefore tractors were the only means of rescue; and all at no charge, another example of Lustleigh team spirit.

The Lustleigh Show has, in its long history, been run by enthusiastic volunteers for the benefit of the residents, friends and families of Lustleigh. Prior to the Second World War and since, there have been literally hundreds of committee members and assistants too many to name, who have made the Show what it is today, and it continues to flourish, enjoyed by thousands of people spanning several generations. Long may it do so.

Chapter 6
LUSTLEIGH NOTABLES

CECIL TORR & YONDER WREYLAND
by Fiona Sutcliffe Maynard

Yonder Wreyland is a property forming part of the Manor of Wreyland, a small hamlet of eight thatched dwellings situated on the outskirts of Lustleigh village. It was the home of Cecil Torr (who was known as the 'scholar squire') and his ancestors during the 18th, 19th and early-20th centuries.

Cecil Torr was born in Mitcham in Surrey in 1857 of Unitarian parents. He was raised in and near London, being educated by a private tutor before going to Harrow. Thereafter, he attended Trinity College, Cambridge, between 1876 and 1880 and left with an 'undistinguished degree'. He was then called to the Bar in 1882 aged 25 and practised (apparently never profitably) as a barrister. Upon inheriting his grandfather's estate at Wreyland, he chose to settle in the West Country.

Torr's love of travel was hereditary; his father (who was a solicitor) developed his son's interest in language and travel throughout his childhood. Although there was no common doctrine, it was his father who presented him to Pope Pius IX and was keen for his son not to waste any opportunity available to him. His father encouraged not only the

Yonder Wreyland, c.1900. The photograph shows William Rice and his second wife Mary (with their daughter Lily) who acted as caretakers during Cecil Torr's many absences from home.

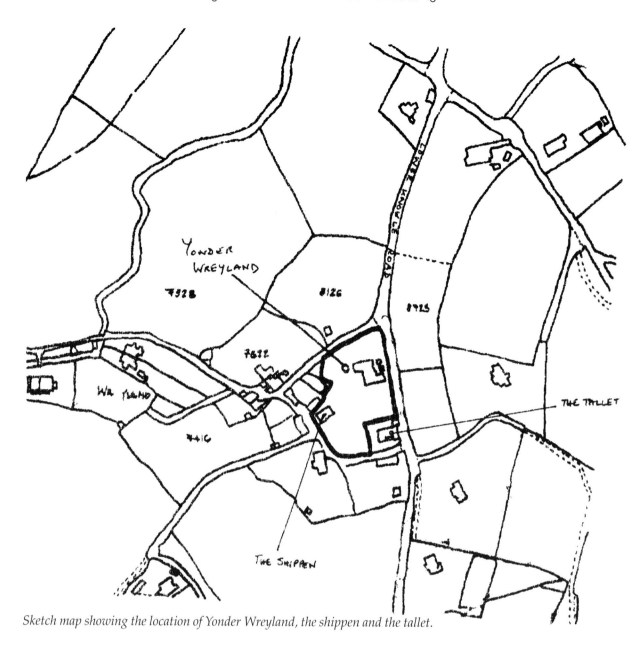

Sketch map showing the location of Yonder Wreyland, the shippen and the tallet.

usual 'good books to read', but also literature such as Continental Bradshaw and Murray's guidebooks – sowing the notions of carefully-planned travel, which ultimately became one of Cecil Torr's chief pleasures. In addition his father told him: 'It would be unprofitable for him to go there until he could talk to people himself in the countries he was visiting.'

Torr's travel diaries between 1867 and 1875 indicate the rigours of his education in this respect, and he records departing from Mitcham via Waterloo or Charing Cross 'by Mail' to Dover and then crossing to Calais. During this period he lists and dates his journeys:

1867 Paris: 10–22 September
1868 Belgium and the Rhine: 11–31 August
1869 Switzerland and Italy: 12 August–3 Sept.
1871 Paris and Switzerland: 15 August–11 Sept.
1872 Belgium and Holland: 19 August–19 Sept.
1873 Austria and Bavaria: 30 July–7 Sept.

1874 Germany and Bohemia: 10 August–4 Sept.
1875 Belgium and France: 25 March–5 April
1875 Germany and Austria: 2 August–3 Sept.

Travelling was not always a comfortable experience and Torr was derisive of modern travelling; the ease and comfort people came to enjoy when they made such trips to Europe in the 20th century. His early recollections were quite different.

Torr became a well-trained and refined scholar of ancient history and language. He used his experiences abroad to good purpose and produced a number of literary books and papers, which challenged previous scholastic reference books and the unreliable foundation on which theories had been constructed. Another legacy Torr inherited from his father was an analytical trait in investigating and judging evidence, both documentary and physical. In *Ancient Ships* (Cambridge University Press, 1895) he comments on certain previous publications as

A day off. The staff of Yonder Wreyland in 1910 – the cook and housekeeper – with George Morecombe in Knowle Road.

being: 'more voluminous than valuable'; in some cases 'careless compilations from those of earlier date'; and as containing 'passing allusions' and 'exaggerations and anachronisms'.

He would scrutinise his subject meticulously, referring to legal texts, old documentary 'inscriptions', and ancient physical material to obtain 'conclusive' testimony, which he cross-checked upon his travels, wherever possible.

Other texts included *Rhodes in Ancient Times* (1885), *Rhodes in Modern Times* (1887), *Memphis and Mycenae* (1896) and *On the Interpretation of Greek Music* (1896). He produced work that rarely allowed subjective comment. However, his views were not constrained if he felt strongly about an issue, and when, for example, alterations to the Church of St John the Baptist in Lustleigh commenced in 1871 he clearly disapproved:

Lavatory tiles replace the granite paving of the chancel, and there is marble of the sort one sees on washstands. It makes one crave for the French system of scheduling old churches as National Monuments, and putting them under the Ministry of Fine Arts.

Torr was a keen antiquarian and a member of several scholarly societies. He took particular interest in the antiquities and ancient customs of his home, and was largely instrumental in reviving the old May Day festivities, which included a treat for the children in the form of a tea. In 1917, there was a shortage of cereals and he tells how he saved the situation with 200 hard-boiled eggs!

His deep roots in Devon enabled him to write true local history; his inherent penetrating observation, both amusing and shrewd, made *Small Talk at Wreyland* truly unique. The text was written originally *sibi et amicis* (for himself and his friends). At Christmas 1916 he was given a book and 'began to write things down'. 'I meant to keep to local matters', he confesses, 'but have gone much further than I meant'. In fact he wrote sufficient for three slim volumes, two of which included photographic plates. He recalls in *Small Talk at Wreyland*:

My great-great-grandfather Nelson Beveridge Gribble was Lord of Wreyland Manor, but always lived in this house – Yonder Wreyland – and never in the Hall House [Hall House was renamed Wreyland Manor in the 1980s]. I believe he held Court Barton 1 and Court Leet 2 and View of Frankpledge 3 in the Lower Parlour here, and it must have been unpleasantly crowded, if Homage 4 and the Tithing 5 came here in full force.

Notes:
1. Court Barton: a civil court held in a manor in which the free tenants or freeholders of the manor were the judges, and the Steward of the manor as the Registrar. It permitted all suits concerning land held within the manor.
2. Homage: tenants knelt before the lord of the manor and said 'I become your man of life and limb' and who were thereby obliged to assist the lord, who would, in turn, protect his tenants. It was abolished by enfranchisement.

Wreyland Manor adopted the 'copyhold' system of tenancy and tenants were answerable to a manor court should they allow their buildings to fall into decay, or remove boundary gates and hedges adjoining neighbouring tenements. The last court to be held at Yonder Wreyland was on 14 February 1871. However, the copyhold tenements developed into freeholds and the manor decayed substantially during Cecil Torr's lifetime, particularly when the Law of Property Act abolished copyhold or 'customary' tenure in 1922.

Various accounts of Yonder Wreyland, its garden, tallet and shippen are given in *Small Talk at Wreyland*; the family's notes, correspondence and photographs are to be found in the Lustleigh Society's Archives Room, and in the Record Office and libraries in Newton Abbot and Exeter.

According to Cecil Torr's notes on Wreyland, reference to Yonder Wreyland is made in a conveyance of the great tithes on the 'messuage, tenement, lands and farm called Wreyland otherwise Yonder Wreyland' on 29 September 1810. Torr makes further comment that Nelson Beveridge Gribble, owner of the Manor of Wreyland and the house Yonder Wreyland, in 1776 had no documents of acquisition or title deeds for the properties and these seem to have either been lost or destroyed. Torr tells us in these notes that:

The Manor of Wreyland includes the neighbouring places on that side of the Wrey, Leigh, Kelly, Wilmead, Knowle and Yeo. It stretches some way further up and down the river and further back across the hill. The manor and tithing are of the same extent.

All buildings of different parts of Wreyland are grouped together in a village. Apparently the names of Lower, Middle, Souther, Forder and Yonder all refer to the buildings of each tenement, and not to the position of its fields.

Yonder Wreyland is constructed of rendered stone and brick under thatch. Three tall cut granite chimneys serve four hearths on the ground floor.

An unusual pose: Cecil Torr in the Scilly Isles. (From Torr's 1916 album)

130

The Pixey Garden at Yonder Wreyland. (From Torr's 1916 album)

Cecil Torr (centre) examines the map before beating the bounds in 1925. He is flanked by the Revd George Rogerson and the Revd Herbert Johnson (Rector of Lustleigh).

Torr's workplace, the tallet. (From Torr's 1916 album)

The shippen. (From Torr's 1916 album)

Following Torr's death in 1928, the main house suffered from a devastating fire in 1929. The house was substantially reconstructed and – at first sight – its external appearance remained true to the original. However, internally much has changed over the years. Some original features still exist, namely the mullion windows in the morning room, and in the hall (formerly known as the 'inner parlour' and likened by one of Torr's friends to 'the kitchen in the Ogre's House' in a pantomime set!) the redressed granite mantel.

In Torr's day, two separate buildings known as the tallet and shippen were sitting rooms. 'Tallet' is a corruption of the Latin 'tabulatum', which means 'upper floor'; and shippen is an Anglo-Saxon derivative of 'scipen' – which means some sort of shed. The former was developed into a cottage in the 1980s, used as holiday accommodation and then sold to the present owners in 1995.

The shippen has been described as a 'ballroom' in the past and despite this pretension, the building does have the benefit of a woodblock floor, although not sprung! True to its former description, it has been used for an autumn and winter series of exercise classes. My predecessor used the shippen as a tearoom when she opened the garden to the public to raise funds for charity. More recently, it has served as a rehearsal space for the Lustleigh Drama Group; and as a party room for my daughter and other children. Planning permission now allows it to be developed into ancillary accommodation to the main house.

The garden benefits from a micro-climate enabling plants which would not normally survive on Dartmoor to flourish. Contrary to the effects of global warming and our changing climate, weather predictions are still based on Cecil Torr's practice:

I find little need of a barometer here. If the wind blows down the valley, the weather is going to be fine. If it blows up the valley, there is going to be wet. And if there is going to be a spell of wet if there is damp upon the hearthstones in the Inner Parlour.

Torr goes on to tell us that most of the old houses had groups of box-edged beds with narrow paths between them, making up some pattern as a whole and these were known as 'pixey gardens': 'As pixies are 12' high, these little paths are pretty much the same to them as Devonshire lanes to human beings.' I have planted a new pixey garden in front of the morning-room window, inspired from old photographs and Torr's writing, and which previously existed here. (There was formerly a draw-well in front of the house but it was filled in before 1839 when this part of the garden was created into *Buxus*.) In the centre of the bed grows a *Cornus controversa* 'Variegata' (wedding cake tree) and thus it seemed appropriate to shape the *Buxus* into hearts

and include four standard 'Felicite Perpetue' roses to represent showers of confetti in the configuration. I ponder from time to time if the 'naked pixies' (Cecil Torr informs us so in *Small Talk, Vol. I*) are united with the pretty fairies under the *Cornus* and dwell in perpetual joy!

Torr planted two olive trees that no longer exist: I have planted another just below the Oval Lawn. In Torr's day, many people around Lustleigh had never seen an olive tree before, and were curious about its fruit, so he gave them olives to try. The comment was: 'Well Mrs **** 'd never have christened her daughter Olive, if her'd a-tasted one of they.'

Despite change, guests from all corners of the world who stay here find the house and garden enchanting. Cecil Torr wrote that Americans were 'much taken with it all', stating that it was worthy of a painting rather than a photograph. Artists do indeed visit and whilst undertaking their task enjoy the beauty and birdsong as Torr's forebears did and as I do now.

PARSON DAVY: 'THE PRINTING PARSON', A TRUE MAN OF GOD
by Veronica Hughes

Lustleigh may not have harboured many famous men but as well as Cecil Torr, another deserves special mention – the Revd William Davy, who was born on 4 March 1743 at Down or Dawn House in Tavistock, the second son of Francis Davy of humble origin. The Davy family moved to Chudleigh and later to Chudleigh Knighton. As a child, William showed many talents, particularly his mechanical and engineering skills, but his parents did not encourage this gift, although it served him well in later life (i.e. his diving bell, printing press, etc.). Records state that on one occasion a mill wasn't functioning properly and Davy made a wooden model which worked well, whereupon he put theory into practice and had the real mill going again, much to the workmen's astonishment!

Davy was educated at Exeter Free Grammar School at the East Gate where he did well, gained good reports and continued to make models to delight his friends. He went up to Balliol College, Oxford, on 30 November 1762 and graduated BA on 28 May 1766. While there, Lord Byron's ideas inspired him to write a series of sermons called 'A System of Divinity' to include all aspects of theology, particularly those on 'Virtues and Vices' of the age. This system comprised 26 octavo volumes, with 500 pages in each volume and 14 copies in all!

Davy was said to be a strong, fine-looking man. He would vault over a gate rather than open it and frequently walked into Exeter and back again to Lustleigh in the same day.

On leaving Oxford he was ordained and appointed to the curacy of Moretonhampstead where he continued his great work. During this curacy he married Sarah Gilbert of Longbrook near Kingsbridge with whom he had four children. His son, Charles, became a clergyman and one daughter survived him. His wife predeceased him by many years.

Davy was a 'perpetual curate' who 'stood-in' for absentee rectors in three parishes at different times. He held curacies in succession at Drewsteignton and Lustleigh, preaching long sermons on 'Virtues and Vices' using Isaiah, Chapter 58, 'Cry aloud, spare not'. Drewsteignton welcomed the sermons on 'Virtues' but strongly objected to those on 'Vices' and complained to the Bishop! However, Drewsteignton's loss became Lustleigh's gain and the Revd moved to the village in 1785 to remain for 40 years. Davy's annual stipend was £40, minus £5 for renting the rectory. He settled down to look after the flock of his absentee rector, the Revd John Mudge, to build the Vestry Room and School House and continue his life's work. As there was then neither a vestry in the church nor a

Parson Davy at the age of 82.

village school, he planned what is now called 'The Old Vestry' to fulfil both these purposes. This building is now an important church property and has many uses.

Lacking finance for his printing endeavours he bought cast-off type from an Exeter printer and constructed a printing press himself in the rectory. That rectory is now the Old Hall and what were probably the remains of the press were discovered in the roof in 1930 after the rectory was sold and became a private dwelling. He printed his sermons himself with the help of his faithful servant Mary Hole, John Hole's wife. Through sheer dedication and determination, and in the face of a lack of both money and encouragement (and worse thanks to some Church dignitaries) he completed the 26 volumes in 1807. Mary Hole, his ever-faithful servant, died in 1808 and richly deserved to be remembered for her valuable part in his work.

While still keeping his curacy, he moved from the rectory to the more comfortable 'Wilmead', a

small farm which his son Charles had bought to the south of the parish. Davy showed much skill as a horticulturist. He created a garden at Wilmead amongst the boulders, planting box, roses, small shrubs and flowers. He planted scriptural texts or moral precepts in box and as the garden was kept under control, the words could easily be deciphered, among them 'Live peaceably', 'Love one another', 'Deal fairly', 'Act wisely', and 'Know thyself'. It is recorded that the Lord's Prayer and the Ten Commandments were also planted in box or shrubs.

Some years before he died, a relative left him some money and at the same time his stipend was increased from £40 to £60 per annum. In 1822 he gave 'a very handsome present of communion plate to the church', as well as a flagon and two patens with the following inscription: 'the gift of Wm. Davy (aged 78) 36 years curate of Lustleigh to that parish for the use of the Sacrament for ever. 1822.' He also founded the 'Davy Charities'.

In 1823 Davy wrote a number of pamphlets on the subject of divinity and, perhaps amazingly, after his previous treatment by the Church hierarchy, they were well received and his massive work was at long last recognised by the then bishop, William Carey, who rewarded him, 'by then a sick old man', with the living of Winkleigh on 22 March 1826. Sadly he died in the vicarage on 13 June having been looked after by his remaining son and daughter until his death. On 17 June 1826 he had his request granted and was buried in the chancel of All Saints Church, Winkleigh. His son, Charles, put the following inscription on the gravestone:

SACRED
TO THE MEMORY
OF
THE REV. WILLIAM DAVY, A.B.,
VICAR OF WINKLEIGH
WHO DIED 13TH JUNE 1826
HE WAS THE AUTHOR OF A SYSTEM OF DIVINITY IN
26 VOLS 8VO.
HIS ZEAL AND LABOUR IN THE WORK OF HIS CALLING
WAS GREAT, PERSEVERING AND SUCCESSFUL.
'HE DIED IN THE FAITH'
'NOR LIFE, NOR DEATH NOR OUGHT BESIDE
FROM GOD THE FAITHFUL SHALL DIVIDE.'

During the restoration of Winkleigh Church in the 1870s the grave and most of the inscription were covered by the installation of seating near the organ. Today such sacrilege seems incredible but nothing it seems is static in this life and apparently not in death. Davy's son Charles later wrote a memoir of him in Volume 1 of *Divinity*. Lustleigh has every reason to be very proud of this remarkable, religious and talented man who is reputed to have been the most renowned theologian of his day. His *System of Divinity* can be seen in the Exeter Cathedral Library and other famous libraries. In conclusion, although Davy received little spiritual or monetary reward except at the end of his life, one assumes that after his death he was welcomed into Heaven with the well-known and loved words, 'well done thou good and faithful servant. Enter thou into the joy of thy Lord.'

Sources
'William Davy, Priest and Printer' by Ursula Radford
    (*Transactions of the Devonshire Association*, 1931, Vol. 13,
    pp325–39)
Western Morning News, 27 March 1949
Lustleigh Guide, 1975
Dictionary of National Biography
Balliol College, Oxford
The History of the Manor and Church of Winkleigh, by Charles
    Worthy, 1876
Revd P. Norman, Vicar of All Saints, Winkleigh.
Notes on Winkleigh Church, 1982

Chapter 7
RANDOM REMINISCENCES

REMINISCENCES
by Various Authors

Collected in this chapter are a wide variety of reminiscences from many different sources but mostly relating to the first half of the 20th century. The chapter concludes with a longer episode, the recollections of John Dray, now a senior resident, who came to Lustleigh as a small boy in 1931.

From the Childhood of a Devon Maid
by Florence Mary Amer

This extract dates from the period before 1914 and was published in the *Parish Magazine, Vol. CVII*, Aug. 1995:

This new home – named Elsford – was in the Bovey Tracey Parish, but our nearest school was about two miles away in the most delightful of Devon villages known as Lustleigh. The four eldest children (Florence was one of a family of 15, 9 boys and 6 girls) were sent there, also some children from the adjoining cottage and from the farm house... Our home was situated high up on the hills and the journey to school was all downhill and rather hard going, through woods, narrow lanes and across several meadows. I am by now 5 years old and so I joined the others in the long trek to school. We had to carry packed food – no school meals or drink in those days. If we needed a drink we had to put our mouths under the tap where we washed our hands... When I was 8½ years old one of my brothers was taken sick and in a lot of pain whilst at school (he was 16 months older than me) so my elder brother and sister told him to go home. Even now I feel very sad at the thought of him going all up over those hills alone over rough tracks.

In those days there was no such thing as free medical service or advice. Indeed ordinary working class folks hesitated to send for a doctor. My parents did what they thought best of course such as a warm bed and hot water bottles but he became rapidly worse and my Father rode nearly four miles to call a doctor. The only means of transport at that time, in the country, was by horse-back – even for the doctor – so about 24 hours later the Dr arrived and at once

ordered my brother to be got to the Cottage Hospital. There being no such thing as an ambulance, our pony was harnessed up and the pony-trap made as comfortable as they could – a mattress and pillows laid in the trap, my brother wrapped in a warm blanket, now in very great pain. He died six days later from a burst appendix and peritonitis; that was in July 1906 when my brother was just ten years old.

There were quite a number of retired Army or Naval Officers and families and other well-to-do people living around the village, and remembering that many of the school children had long distances to walk to school in all kinds of weather they decided to buy up a consignment of felt slippers for the use of us to change into when our feet were very wet and cold. The heating of our school was by large round iron stoves, fired by coke, and with high strong fire guards. The school consisted of one large room and two smaller ones. The infants, aged from five to about six and a half in room one, those from that age up to nine in room 2; from that age we were all in the large main room – Standards 2, 3, 4 & 5. The schoolmaster taught all these. A lady teacher in charge of Standard 1 and a lady with the infants. The school leaving age up to approximately 1909 was 13 years. Some children could leave at 12 years if their parents could get what was then known as a Labour Certificate. I left school when I was 13.

There was also the problem – when we left school – for our parents to find suitable jobs for us. Usually the boys were taken on the farms and 'lived-in' with the farmer and family, partly I suspect because they were always on call, early mornings and late evenings, for a very small wage. The parents were thankful enough though, partly because it relieved the congestion at home, and the few shillings they earned helped to buy their boots and clothes. The girls either entered domestic service or worked as shop assistants, or if the parents could afford it put to learn dress making. For a year or two after I left school I was sent to live with my paternal grand-parents who were quite old and really needed help. Then I became a shop assistant in Lustleigh village earning 5/- (25 pence) a week plus my Board and Lodge where I remained until October 1918, just before my marriage.

From the Book of Memories of Anna Aston

(née Bunclarke, born in Lustleigh, 1929, now living in Torquay)

1940–46. Mr Osborne had a bonfire and fireworks for all Brookfield children on the land where the railway carriage is; he lets this out in the summer to visitors. Mr Osborne owns the bakery and has sons Charlie, George, Walter and daughter Brenda. They have a Christmas tree outside of their window planted when the children were small; now quite big. Bert Moore sits at the post box in his wheel chair talking to all the people who come to post letters. Old Andrews walks about the village in his tail coat, now green with age. He lives at the Mill with Mrs Moors and Harry. Gran keeps Brookside, a guest house opposite the Cleave Hotel run by Mrs Paynter who has one blue eye and one brown like Lady Hamilton; she dresses up as her at the Fancy Dress Balls held in the Conservative Club.

The searchlight unit was stationed at Sanduck and was run by a man called Neiburg. I talked to him a lot and learned quite a bit about the workings of it. A land-mine dropped on the bridge at Caseley and overturned a carrier (Army) that was passing under and killed him. We had one barrage balloon at Lustleigh (Pepperdon). The Kelly Mine closed because it was being run by a German syndicate. In fact in the war years Lustleigh was a hive of excitement, no more the serene peaceful village, everything a real bustle. Then after the war all back to normal, or could it ever be? Women were more independent as they had had to do men's jobs. So men came back from the war and found women's outlooks had changed; no more were they going to stay at home and just house-keep and have children; they wanted more money and wanted to work in Newton Abbot or Bovey Tracey.

In the war men who were too old or disabled formed the Home Guard (or LDV as it was first called). I joined the Junior Red Cross and even had to man stirrup pumps. We had rehearsals of bomb victims on the village green. Then the Yanks came, what a day and excitement that was. When the first Yanks came into Lustleigh to shop they thought they were Germans because of their helmets and called out the Home Guard. It took a lot of persuasion for the villagers to pass them as Yanks.

Lustleigh Fire Guards, 1943

by Mr Lionel Morecombe

A one-time Lustleigh resident, Lionel Morecombe presented a silver cup inscribed 'Lustleigh Fire Guards, 1943' to the Lustleigh Society in 1991. The *Mid Devon Advertiser* of 18 May 1943 reported that

Lustleigh was showing 'the rest of the rural area a wonderful example in Fire Guard Organisation'. The extent of their training was revealed 'when their three teams competed for a cup which had been presented by an anonymous friend.' Lionel Morecombe explained (as he had done in the *Parish Magazine, Vol. CXIII, p.90*) that:

The competition was clearly no walkover, there were 5 or 6 teams competing; the winning team (who received the cup) consisted of Bill Hatherly, Phyllis Morecombe and Kathleen Chetwynd. A special three-sided structure was built in the cricket field – the 4th side was left open so that the judges could see what was happening inside. Bill Hatherly, it appears, was an ingenious designer and produced – in the workshop attached to his cider press – a special elongated handle for the nozzle of his stirrup pump (the standard fire fighting equipment of the day – every house was equipped with at least one) so that he could tackle the fire without exposing himself to unnecessary danger.

Reminiscences of Nearly 50 Years Ago

by the late Misses Raikes (Betty and Joan)

The following was printed in the *Parish Magazine*, December 1994:

There are others who lived in Lustleigh before and during the war – we only came in 1945. We remember that the Thanksgiving Service on VE Day had to be timed so as not to clash with a pre-arranged performance of Pygmalion *by the Lustleigh Players, as parishioners would want to attend both. We remember the very warm welcome given to us as newcomers, and also the generous Welcome Home cheques given to those returning from the Forces, even if they had only been in Lustleigh for a matter of months.*

Those were the days when Lustleigh had its resident policeman, and District Nurse (who refused to take her holiday while an elderly patient was terminally ill); and the school was still flourishing in what is now Old School House. All the schoolchildren used to troop merrily across the road to Church House for excellent dinners, cooked in the kitchen which was later used for Meals-on-Wheels for Lustleigh, Bovey, Moreton and beyond.

The train still ran. The guard and passengers would wait patiently for the latecomer hurrying over the bridge and down the steps to catch the 7.59a.m. train; in the evening the guard got out at all the halts to hang up oil lamps, which he then collected on the last train back into Newton, and whenever there was a stretch of single line track, the engine-driver had to

The Parson's Loaf on Mapstone Hill; why it is so called remains a mystery.

Looking west, the Mill Leat and Mill Lane to the left. The road to Rudge is straight ahead.

collect a 'Staff', which he carried to prove that his was the only train on the line. Mothers used to take their babies in their prams by train to Bovey, to the Baby Clinic, and the last train from Newton was timed to allow folk to return from the latest house in the cinema.

The Doctors held their surgeries in the Bibbings' dining room (now Stable House Gallery) or in the house today called Columbine, with patients waiting outside in the open in all weathers; prescriptions had to be taken to the chemist by the patient, until it was arranged to send medicines down, first to an open shelf in the Churchyard, later to an unlocked cupboard on Church House wall. The new Doctor's Surgery in the Old Vestry was partly paid for by grateful patients.

Before the days of television, there were many social activities in the then Conservative Hall (now the Village Hall) and in Church House: dances, whist drives, badminton, Scouts, Guides, Brownies and more; and at Christmas the village children's party. The first Flower Shows on Bank Holiday in early August and in late October in the Conservative Hall, the autumn one particularly memorable for the colour and fragrance of chrysanthemums and apples; in those early days the Horticultural Society's bank balance was so modest that the Treasurer had

to give surety for an overdraft when drawing out the prize money.

On Plough Sunday, the first Sunday after Twelfth Night, a farmer (and there were many more farms worked then) brought a small plough into Church and in broad Devon dialect asked the Rector to bless the plough and all the work in the fields in the coming year; at the Rogation Sunday evening service, Rector, Choir and congregation would process through the village, and sing hymns and say prayers along the way.

At the Coronation in 1953, parishioners gathered for an 8 am service, most relieved that the WI seat had arrived safely, and thrilled that Everest had been climbed. Hugh Ruttledge, a member of the 1933 Everest expedition lived in the village. During Coronation Day morning, all Lustleigh children were given Coronation mugs, and in the evening many folk climbed up to a big bonfire by the Nutcracker Rock and watched the beacons lit on surrounding hilltops. That was the year that village opinion was deeply divided over the retention or removal of the elm trees round the church; as it was later over the stars painted on the chancel ceiling.

There were more shops then: Bibbings' grocery store, a Co-op with a butcher once a week where the Dairy now is, the Bakery, confectioners near Bridge

Two photographs of the 'animil' of 1947.
(from *Widecombe in the Moor* by Stephen Woods)

House and at the present Columbine; the Post Office sold a larger number of garden and household items and haberdashery as well; the Primrose Cottage sold hardware and had a petrol pump, and there was a forge opposite the beautiful topiary-arched gateway of Bickley. Milk was dispensed by Mr and Mrs Reed from Bishopstone and later by Joan and Eddie Ellis from one of the Rock Cottages. Mr May had a nursery garden in Caseley Lane.

We shall never forget the amazing Animil (a Dartmoor term for a thin coating of ice – singularly beautiful; from the Old English Ammel [enamel] – JMR) of 1947 when the snow coated the branches of the trees, thawed and froze again, leaving each twig encased in ice which tinkled in the breeze, pale pink and gold at sunrise and sunset. Many things have changed in the last fifty years but Lustleigh continues to be a friendly, deeply caring village.

Jean Wills Sorts Out Family Relationships

In 1912 Scott and Lilian Thorn Painter ran the Cleave and Florence Mary Thorn Painter, a niece of Scott, then aged 14, worked in the Cleave. Arthur John Allin, a carpenter and builder (who was known as Jack) married Florence. Florence and Jack lived in the cottage on the green which Jack restored from a condemned building. Their three children were called Kathleen Mary Allin, Dorothy Allin and David John Allin; they were baptised and confirmed in the Parish Church and all three went to school in Lustleigh. Later Kathleen was married in Lustleigh Church to Warrant Officer Robert John Chisholm. Their children were called Anne, Dorothy, Jean and Robert. The last two still live in the village. Jean married David Wills, the son of Earnest George Wills who lived at Tottiford by Hennock. Both Earnest and his brother Alfie Wills went to Lustleigh school. Jean and David's children are called Emma, Francis, Mary and William Robert George. Emma Wills was May Queen in 2000.

Mrs Iris Gould (late of Nutcombe) Sheds Light on the Origins of the Gould Memorial Lantern on the Churchyard Wall

The following is an extract from the *Parish Magazine* of October 1994:

The memorial lamp , on its granite plinth, was erected by his family to commemorate the life and work of James Nutcombe Gould (1849–1899). James grew up

at Knowle House, one of a family of 13. After his marriage he and his wife Edith lived for a time at Lower Combe House and more latterly at Well Park. He was a distinguished amateur actor, having many times appeared on the London stage with his friend Henry Irving. In 1879 he founded a theatrical company which he called 'The Barn Owls', consisting largely of his brothers and sisters and their friends; this company met with considerable success because their performances raised sufficient money to fund the installation of the organ and the central heating in our parish church.

A Memory of 60 Years Ago
by Myles Bowen of Rudge

A mother and her 4-year-old child were evacuated from London in September 1939 but returned to London in November of the same year, the expected Blitz having not yet transpired. One summer day in 1999 – 60 years later – the afore-mentioned child, now in his sixties, appeared, complete with wife, outside Rudge. Considering his age at the time he had remarkably clear memories of his stay in Lustleigh. He asked about Ned Wills and was able to visit him. He remembered old farmer Wills (Ned's father) shooting a fox in the back yard through the window – glass and all! He also recalled how the farm's carthorse, a notorious escaper, had managed to get from his stable, going round the back of the cattle byre, to where an upstairs door led into a loft used as a feed store; on entering all four of his feet went through the rotten floor! Our evacuee clearly remembered the four huge shaggy legs hanging down from the ceiling! The horse was apparently recovered without serious injury.

GROWING UP IN THE THIRTIES
by John Dray

Some of the older residents of the village, including myself, are apt to say from time to time, 'people that never knew Lustleigh prior to 1945, are not real Lustleigh people.' I know this may make me sound a bigot, but with all due respect, those who did not know Lustleigh in those halcyon days during the years of the 1920s and '30s, cannot imagine what it was like living in this village. The war brought about such a rapid social change in such a short time. A lot of young men and women that had gone off to the war never returned and I do not mean they had all become casualties, but some had married or found employment in other parts of the country, and others who did return were not prepared to settle back into the old drudgery of farm and other menial and manual work. Their fathers may have done so after the Great War but that was not for them, so they looked elsewhere for work, and whereas nearly all the men and women of the village worked for their living in the village prior to the war, by 1947–48 most found work outside the village. Beside the determination to find better jobs and other means of earning a living, the desire to have a better standard of living was also in demand and thence started the great scramble for money and more and better possessions. Good or bad, I pass no judgement, but that is what closed the door on the old village way of life. It was not only in Lustleigh this happened, but all over the country, all over the world come to that. That, readers, is why Lustleigh is so changed from the days of my boyhood.

My growing up was through the 1930s; during those years there were family names that had been in the village for many generations and one would imagine they would continue to be around for many to come. There were Bunclarkes, Parkers, Aggetts, Horrells, Waldrons and many others, all now gone. Not all have died out, but as I have already mentioned, many have gone off to seek their living in other parts of the wide world.

A big blow to village and community life came with the closure of the school, as in my day, practically all the village children went to that school. They started as infants and left as adults ready to find employment and earn their living. Some who were able to pass the entrance examination were able to go on to Newton Abbot Grammar school, but they left at 16, so [it was] no great academic advantage. The reason why the closing of the school was a bad thing was because with all the children going to the same school, there was a bonding between them. Each knew the other's name, each knew where the other lived, where the fathers worked or how they made their living, so you see, we became in a way like an extended family. We more or less all had the same standard of living and sharing was the general thing among us. I cannot recall a greedy child or bully among those I attended school with. If there was a squabble, as there was occasionally, it was soon forgotten and no one was missed when the sweets were handed around.

We were taught the subjects required by the National Curriculum and, in addition, the boys were taught gardening and the girls were sent off to Bovey Tracey once a week to be taught domestic science, cooking in other words. There were no biology classes, but the children knew from a very early age that copulation must take place between a male and female before birth can happen. They learnt this in a natural healthy way from observation of beasts and birds around them. Consequently, sex, as these things are constantly referred to these days, was not a secret taboo. No doubt there were some 'Cider with Rosy' ventures from time to time, but that was not considered a crime.

The school and Sunday school gave us an outing to the seaside each year, the school to Teignmouth, the Sunday school to Paignton. On the school trip we were taken by charabancs, a great adventure. An interesting mode of transport was provided for the mothers. A Mr George Beer who owned the coal yard had a large lorry that he used for delivering the coal, which he also used for animal transport, by fixing slatted wooded sides and back. Come outing day, a small body complete with seats was bolted to the flat bed, and hey presto, it became a small coach. How many mums it carried I cannot remember, but it must have been about 20. We all set off to the seaside, another adventure for the children of the village. At the seaside we ate a mixture of ice-cream, winkles and candyfloss, which was capped by a cream tea provided as part of the treat. Can you wonder that a lot of the children were not so lively on the homeward journey as on the outward run? The Sunday school outing was much the same as the school trip, but travelling by train. In the summer time trains from Moretonhampstead ran through to Goodrington with no change. The choir boys also had an outing and I remember one such outing as being taken to Totnes and then going down the Dart by boat and homeward from Kingswear by train. I have repeated that journey several times since, but none gave the same magical feelings as that first trip.

Another outing if one may call it such, was a family 'do' where Mum, Dad and the children, all carrying some item required for a picnic, would make their way down to Boveycombe Weir. This was reached by going up the lane at the top of Pethybridge, through Heaven's Gate and following a clear track down to the River Bovey. At the riverside in those days was quite a nice little sandy beach and on the far side was about an acre of short, soft grass. On a warm Sunday there would be about half a dozen families at least, all there to enjoy a picnic in surrounding beauty, second to none in this wide world. The children would play in the river [which was] much deeper then as there was a dam across. The water was about three feet deep in places, but quite safe. Fathers would gather sticks and light fires to boil the kettle carried from home, to make tea. Mothers would spread the tablecloth and lay out the 'goodies' baked and prepared for this special occasion, then silence would reign when the frolicking children gathered to devour the spread. It was then home very happy and very tired and early to bed with no protest.

So what did we children do for recreation and pleasure, having no television or family motor cars? Well there was a good lively Scout and Cub pack for the boys and a Guide and Brownie pack for the girls to start with – great fun – and those who have not sat around a camp fire singing and drinking cups of hot cocoa have not lived, the same applies to camping. Sometimes the camps were only in a field in the village, but at other times we would join other packs as far afield as Ogwell. I remember what an adventure it was, sleeping, washing and eating with the days spent playing various sports and learning the ways of Scouting. There were also domestic chores to be done such as potato peeling, etc. Every summer Scout packs from far-off places came to Lustleigh for their annual camp, often camping in a field at Lower Coombe and sometimes at Higher Coombe. We were always invited to join them on campfire nights and the memories of those occasions remain with me to this day.

At least a dozen village boys were in the church choir, three pence a service and weddings and funerals brought a bonus of two shillings and six pence. Worth joining! We also had a 'kick around football team' – in other words not a very good one. We played most villages around, and confess the game usually finished 10-0 against us. But it was great fun and we were always happy to meet other lads from outside.

We also had a school cricket team [and we were] not too bad at that sport. Some will remember the late Bill Amery, and think of him as rather portly in stature; in fact he was one of the best players in the school team in my days and kept the fielders constantly on the run.

A train puffed up the line that ran through the village those days, it ran between Newton Abbot and Moretonhampstead. The times of arrival up and down at Lustleigh were very convenient I seem to remember. Give and take a quarter of an hour, one went down in the morning at around 8.00a.m., one came up around 1.00p.m., another down at 2.00p.m. and up again at 5.00p.m., so you see those working in the fields about and not possessing a watch knew just when it was starting and finishing time. There were other trains beside the ones I mention, but recalling the first down train reminds me of times which will make readers smile, when I tell you of an oft occurrence.

For a few years I lived in Brookside so saw what I am about to relate often. There were a number of young girls, my sister Kathleen was one, who worked in Newton Abbot in shops and offices and travelled to and fro on the trains. Like all young girls, they seemed to be reluctant to get up in the morning. I had better be careful, but it's true, especially if there had been a dance in the village or close by the previous evening. As a consequence, often as the train pulled out of the station, they would be late, running along the path from the Cleave to the station. The driver and guard knew they should be aboard so would be on the checkout for them. When spotted the train would squeak to a halt, the guard would clamber down and the girls would be bundled aboard. [There is] something to be said for the old world; as I say, it was always give and take a little, even on train timetables.

Another benefit from having a train service was that children from the village could go up to Moretonhampstead to the Rex Cinema on Saturday mornings. The cinema was an old Territorial Drill Hall in Ford Street, long since gone. We children thought it the world's greatest, but my wife Grace, who during the war was stationed in Moreton with the Women's Land Army and who had come from London and other girls from other big cities, referred to it as 'The Bug Hutch' and other derogatory names; they little knew the pleasure that place brought to the country folk around. I done rather well as the Manager come Projectionist came from Lustleigh, and for sticking up a few posters I got a ticket for the next week's show.

During the winter months, children would read, paint or make things from any materials they could get their hands on. I remember that even when I lived in Brookside in 1937 there was no electricity and in many other houses in the village, until after the war, some like Higher Coombe had their own generators, but not a mains supply. I mention this because I remember doing what I thought was a good painting in the light of our oil lamps, and the next morning when I viewed it in daylight the colours were all different to what they had been the night before.

A children's library came to the village once a week and I remember the kindly lady librarian explaining the contents of some of the books so that we could make our choice. She had a lovely reading voice like two other women I knew, my mother and one lady teacher. Through these three ladies, I developed a love of books still with me and by coincidence I married a book lover, and we regard sitting in a comfy chair with a good book one of the pleasures in life.

Each season brought its own pleasures. Towards autumn there were masses of big juicy blackberries to gather, hazel and chestnuts unlimited. Mushrooms could be gathered by the basket full. There was a sale for these in the village, and the coppers that resulted were not spent on sweets but were put aside to purchase fireworks later.

You, I hope, will think that the children did not fare too badly in those days, but what of the parents? Farming was of course the main source of income for many of the menfolk of the village, and for quite a lot of others it was the gardening at the 'big houses' – Kelly, Rudge, Hisley, Ellimore, South Harton, North Harton, Sanduck and Mapstone, with even a family of Chudleys farming out of Bickley in the middle of the village; the land they farmed was up Mapstone road beyond the big rock. These were all active and productive farms, all employing local men and sometimes women to help with the domestic chores. A variety of crops were grown both for human and animal foods, all work being done by human and horse power. There was not one tractor in Lustleigh before the war and not many until some time after.

The livestock they kept were mainly cattle, the beautiful South Devons, great for both meat and milk production. Sheep – Devon Long Wools – were very docile and easy to contain. Some of the breeds today can jump a five-bar gate. All had a yard full of hens so eggs galore, and of course a pig or two. These were not so much to sell, but to keep the larder well stocked with bacon and ham. At least four farmers I remember had a milk round, which I suppose was a staple part of their income. Lovely milk those South Devons gave and [the] cream [was] the best in the world – take my word for that. The hedges were always cut and regularly layered and pared, as they say in Devon. No need for miles of sheep netting and worst still wretched barbed wire; an old gentleman once said to me that he that invented barbed wire should have been hung with the wretched stuff. [A] bit drastic, but understandable, for he had been in the Boer War where it was first used and then had seen what it could do to men in the Great War.

The hay from the meadows in those days was the best, full of best grass, herbs and other nutritious plants, all now gone with the massive doses of nitrates they get these days. Those same hay fields before being cut would be covered with clouds of lovely butterflies and the hedgerows were full of singing birds, many of which I never see now. What has gone wrong? What have we done?

Most of the farms had productive orchards and in the autumn wagon loads of apples were seen moving through the village on their way to Kelly Farm, where they were pressed into cider, always provided in the harvest fields and on other thirst-creating occasions.

I have mentioned the drudgery of a lot of the work to be done on a farm, one prime example was potato digging, all done by hand. Imagine walking into a four-acre field and knowing it was your task to dig the potatoes therein. The potatoes had to be sorted and put into trenches, covered in straw and then earthed over to store until required. These were called 'Teddy Clamps', the teddy referring to the King Edward potato of that name and very popular. Often it would rain and the digger would drape a sack over his back and carry on digging. There was no hot shower or bath to go home to, as few if any working-class cottages had such luxuries in those days. Soul destroying without a doubt.

There were job spin offs from the farming industry; with such a large amount of horses required, the local smith was kept very busy and the sound of the anvil ringing was a constant sound wherever you were in the village. Often there were two or three horses awaiting their turn to be shod, tied up on the hedge opposite the smithy (there was no opening there in those days). Another benefactor was the thatcher, as not only were many farmhouses, barns and cottages thatched, but most of the hay and corn was ricked when harvested. The ricks needed thatching to keep them dry until the thrashing machine made its rounds which could be up to six months or more.

In those days there were multitudes of rabbits every-where, and to avoid crop damage and as an income the farmers often sold the trapping rights to professional trappers, who would use the now illegal gin traps, catching 100 plus a night – at six pence each not bad, but it was a short season, something like August till March, between those months the rabbit was out of season. Most men in the village kept a ferret and one way or the other would keep his table supplied. Rabbit was in fact their main meat diet; [it is] surprising the tasty dishes that can be made from rabbit by a good cook and the ladies of Lustleigh were among the best. Something that readers may find hard to believe is that those days and up to the 1940s, one could take a dead rabbit wrapped with brown paper around its belly and suitably addressed to the Post Office, and post it to anywhere in the British Isles and it would be safely delivered.

Before I close this brief account of my knowledge of the Lustleigh I grew up in, I must mention the village itself. In the village centre, little has changed. The building now known as the Primrose Café was then a low, thatched structure, in which goods were stored for the adjacent shop, the Old Post Office, known to us as 'Bibbings', Bibbings being the owners throughout that time. This shop was where the 'haves' shopped, selling the same goods as the Co-op, which was housed in the building now known as The Dairy, but charging twice the price. The Co-operative Store, to give it the correct title, was where the 'have-nots' shopped, for things were cheaper, and one could have them on tick until the next pay day; it was no laugh in those days. This store was very popular with the lady shoppers also, as it was a meeting place where all the village gossip was gathered and exchanged. None were in a hurry to get served and none were served in a hurry, as the manager was only too happy to join in the gossip. 'Woe betide any young lady seen with a few blades of grass adhering to the back of her coat.'

The Post Office was much as today, but as telephones were not so numerous in those days, urgent messages were sent by telegram and lucky was the boy who happened to be around when one arrived at the PO because he would get half a crown to deliver it, and often a shilling from the recipient. He would be King for the day, with many friends and much advice as to how best to spend his fortune.

This brings me to THE shop, run by a Miss Eliza Easton, a rendezvous for all children that found themselves wealthy with a few coppers to spend. It is the house next to the old smithy, now called Columbine, where generations of children have spent hours, mulling over which sweets to spend their money on.

In the annexe to the Gospel Chapel the local Postman had a boot and shoe-repair shop and also cut gents' hair, a painful operation I still remember, as the hand clippers always needed sharpening when it came to my turn. At the foot of the railway bridge by the stream, there was a small grocery shop and at the top of Brookfield a bakery. This bakery had a donkey which pulled a small cart delivering bread and I recall on numerous occasions hearing yells from the baker, when the wretched beast, half way up Mapstone Hill, decided to go home hell for leather. There was as always the Cleave Hotel, then ran by a Mr Painter for many years. To us boys he was a very nice man, as whenever we saw him, he would pull from his waistcoat pocket, cigarette cards, always prized by small boys. Various butchers, bakers and general stores from Moretonhampstead and Bovey Tracey made delivery rounds, which saved the expense and time of shopping elsewhere.

That then is how it was, and how I knew it, growing up in Lustleigh in the good old days as some would say – others may not – take your choice.

Chapter 8

A MILLENNIUM VIEWPOINT

MILLENNIUM PHOTOGRAPHIC PROJECT: 'PICTURE ME'

by Elliot Bialick

The parish of Lustleigh extends further than I ever realised, and in it live some 700 people. The idea of a photographic record of every person in the community seemed particularly apt in the millennium year. I trust it is no less so as the project spans the year following and seems unlikely to be complete until the year 2002, or even later.

I regard it as important that in taking photographs I should be no more than a recorder. The idea for the image must come from the individual being photographed; hence the title of

this project. I want to give every subject the opportunity to represent him or herself as they wish to be seen in a visual record of this time. Some have elected to be shown at their work, others at leisure, at home, or pursuing a task or hobby. I have been amazed and delighted at the diversity of skills and interests which are represented; these – as much as the participants themselves – provide a valuable archive for posterity.

I began taking photographs as a teenager in the 1960s. Looking back at prints from that era I see so many changes; not only in the main subjects but also in their surroundings and the small incidental details that are caught in camera which provide an insight into customs of the period. Already children whom I have photographed for 'Picture Me' have grown into adolescents and, sadly, at the other end of the scale, some people are no longer with us.

Anne Beaumont designed this stained-glass panel in her front door.

Dave Wills delivers warmth and comfort.

Alan Beare prepares to dive.

Kirsty Moore explains the finer points of her favourite soup recipe.

Hilary Gould digs for victory in her garden.

Dr David Connell reading outside Lower Wreyland.

Paul Angus rows and rows and rows.

Above: *Joan Ellis baking one of her renowned cakes.*

Right: *Kenric Foster walked his dog Cassie down Mapstone Hill for 20 years.*

Below: *Margaret Burgoyne age 92 and at age 5.*

The decision to use a digital camera for the project has led to my not being constrained by film or processing costs, and this is a tremendous boon. It also means that for the more camera-shy of my sitters I can take lots of pictures, only finishing when there is one with which they are pleased.

When complete, the images will be recorded on a compact disc and made available to anybody who wants a copy. I hope that all the images will fit onto a single disc. It will be possible to view the disc on a monitor using any recent computer. Also, I hope to have an exhibition of all the images in the Village Hall so that everyone may have a chance of seeing the final 'Picture Me' archive.

My sincere thanks to the 200 or more who have (at the time of writing, May 2001) afforded me the opportunity to take their photograph. All others can expect to receive a call shortly.

THE LUSTLEIGH MILLENNIUM YEAR
by Patrick Barker, Secretary to the (now defunct) 2nd Millennium (ad-hoc) Committee

Early in 1999 the Parish Council suggested that Lustleigh village should celebrate the year 2000 and perhaps interested people could be found to suggest, organise and run events, memorials, parties or other events that would take place throughout the year. The then Parish Council Chairman, Hugh Gould, approached numerous people; how these were selected remains a mystery, and thus the 2nd Millennium Committee was born.

The initial meetings of this committee went unrecorded but the offer by William and Teresa Bavin of the House of Marbles to manufacture a 'one off' design of a glass mug or paperweight that would be presented to all children of the parish who were under 18 on 1 January 2000 was very easy to accept. Other ideas were to involve all possible village clubs and/or committees and to hold a street party or main event of some form on Midsummer's Day.

The first recorded meeting was on 18 March 1999 and took place at Bow Cottage. By this time the House of Marbles had produced samples of paperweights and glass mugs (the glass mug was chosen) and ideas for other events and fund-raising were well under discussion. These included being part of the British Beacon event, a Red Cross sponsored walk, a time capsule, the re-opening of the village well and a maypole seat as a permanent memorial. All of these events (with the exception of the glass mugs) eventually never took place, but research for them provided much activity. Only one villager asked Patrick Barker and John Halsey why they were digging 5' holes in the Green, and no, they never did find the supposed site of the old well.

Fund-raising now became a focus and on 26 April 1999 the Parish Council granted £500 towards millennium events. Additionally a 50/50 auction was planned and it was suggested that the committee should apply for a millennium grant from the National Lottery. Unfortunately, the committee being on an 'ad-hoc' basis and therefore having no constitution or bank account, it was unable to apply for lottery monies. The 50/50 auction took place on 26 June 1999 in the Cleave by kind permission of Alison Perring and proved to be a wild success. It seemed that most of the village attended and with Dave Wills as the auctioneer £622.15 was raised.

On 10 November 1999 the Lustleigh Show Committee unanimously voted £1000 towards the millennium events and with this the fund-raising was largely completed. By 15 November 1999 events and plans for the millennium year had been nearly completed. The idea of a granite maypole rock with a seat had to be abandoned due to cost and was replaced with the idea of a new boundary stone that would be positioned during the next beating of the bounds due to take place in 2000. The 'street party' idea had by now escalated, and was planned to include major daytime events, a children's party and an evening charity ball to be organised by Lustleigh Cricket Club. The idea for a community party in the Village Hall on 31 December had unfortunately met with little response and was abandoned. Instead a celebration of Christianity would take place in the church and this, together with a torch-lit procession heralded by fireworks, would bring in the new millennium.

On 31 December 1999 the first organised village event took place commencing with a celebration of Christianity held in the church with the kind permission of the Parochial Church Council and organised by Anna Robertson. It seemed that the entire village was there to hear the amazing variety of music, hymns and readings by parishioners that comprised this celebration with standing room only for the latecomers. This, followed by the mulled wine served on the church steps by Henry Reddaway and his helpers, provided an excellent start to the New Year's Eve celebrations. Following a torch-lit procession around the village centre culminating in the cricket field, the fireworks display commenced with a dozen rockets at five minutes to midnight, to be followed by community singing, then another dozen rockets together at midnight, and again a final dozen rockets at five minutes after midnight – at least that was the plan. With Dave Wills as the 'Master of Fireworks' and Patrick Barker as his assistant, the first 12 rockets shot skywards and exploded as planned. The next 12, designed to explode all together did exactly that – but at ground level – leaving Patrick surrounded by smoke and providing a most satisfactory 'bang' which, according to the village children, was the 'best yet'. The last 12

Vintage motor cars join the Millennium Parade in front of Primrose Cottage.

Church House sports the Union flag for the Millennium Fayre.

Midsummer's Day, 24 June 2000. A happy day for all, blessed with sunshine.

Millennium Fayre, 2000; entertaining the crowds in front of the medieval 'Cleavage Arms'.

climbed into the air a little raggedly but completed a most excellent and memorable evening.

The next day, 1 January 2000, with no blackouts, water cuts or any of the other disasters happening that were supposed to occur as a result of the 'millennium bug', the millennium tankards were distributed to 129 children of the parish who were under the age of 18 on this date.

By 6 March 2000 plans for the Lustleigh Millennium Fayre to be held on 24 June 2000 were well under way with a new committee led by Don Badger. Don commented:

In my opinion, the days of the old-fashioned style street party have gone and, furthermore, I cannot imagine residents wanting to sit around eating jelly and custard whilst being watched, photographed or filmed by visitors.

Having expressed his opinion, Don was immediately 'offered' the job of Chairman and 'requested' to organise the day.

Lustleigh May Day Committee offered its own lasting tribute to commemorate the new millennium. This was in the form of a new throne on the May Queen's rock in the village orchard, designed by local architect Doug Cooper and carved out of granite from Blackenstone Quarry, Moretonhampstead, by Master Mason Waren Pappas. The design of the throne was kept secret until officially unveiled on Monday 1 May 2000 by Lustleigh's oldest surviving May Queen, Mrs Nell Squires, followed by a barbecue and picnic.

On 27 May 2000 the quinquennial beating of the bounds took place with about 20 plus parishioners attending the two-day stroll. Young five-year-old Daisy Wright carried off the record for the youngest person ever to complete the course and the Reverend Bob Leigh highlighted the event with the blessing of the new boundary stone. The 'millennium rock' is sited at the point where the parish boundary crosses the Green Lane, which runs from the Manaton Road to Hisley Bridge and where the parish boundary emerges from Pullabrook Wood.

Plans for the Millennium Fayre were by now in an advanced stage. These included closing the centre of the village to traffic and taking it back in time by dressing it like a film set. The closed area would be from the bottom of Mapstone Hill through to Mill Lane and would include Lustleigh School, the Cleave, the Village Green, Primrose Cottage, Lustleigh Dairy, the Post Office, Orchard Garage, the Village Hall and the Orchard. Rather then portray just one period, the aim would be to try to show

Lustleigh through the ages; the scene is set for the Millennium Fayre.

Lustleigh through the ages, from the turn of the last millennium through the Middle Ages, the coming of the age of steam, through the World Wars to the present day. It was envisaged that the Fayre would include a street market, a thatched alehouse, street entertainers and period musicians, together with old agricultural machinery, a collection of old vehicles from different periods and a Town Crier. There would also be a children's party held in the Orchard and the Cricket Club would hold an evening charity ball sited in a large marquee on the cricket pitch with live music and dinner.

On 23 June 2000, the day before 'THE DAY' dawned clear and bright. Final preparations were being made, the thatched alehouse was nearing completion, tents were going up, signs were being hammered into the ground, the hog-roast cooker was fetched, the church was being decorated, as were the school, the Dairy and Village Hall, bunting had been made and hung, a flagpole with a massive Union Jack positioned on Flagpole Rock, old farm implements were fetched and positioned, costumes had been made, hired or sourced, and finally all was ready, or so we thought. Don, however, had more ideas, new ideas, fresh ideas that resulted in more flags, more bunting and more signs.

Saturday 24 June 2000 – Midsummer's Day – 'The Day The Village Partied'. The stage was set, the players primed and finally it was 'action Lustleigh'. With the roads closed, Molly and Justin Amery's fields filling up with cars, market stalls set up in the village centre, steam traction engines in place and various collectors' vehicles dotted around the village, the events started with the Lustleigh School giving a Victorian concert on the Village Green. Jane Dennis, Trish Roberts and Sandy French, together with the children of Lustleigh School, had also produced a time-line of the history of Lustleigh with the school dressed in the period of Queen Victoria's Jubilee (1887) and were also running a 'Paint Queen Victoria' competition, making Victorian greeting cards and giving a demonstration of copperplate handwriting.

The fortune-teller, Doctor Dee (alias David Connell) was in his tent on the Green, next to the 'guess the weight of the lamb' competition when the 'History of the World' (in 15 minutes) was performed in the Orchard by John King and his Pierrot Troupe – Joely Badger, Lisa Howarth, Ned Gould and Jack Webb. The church was open with a Flower Festival and a 'Celebration of Christenings' on show ably organised by Julia Vittle, together with an Old Nun (Hilary Gould) running around the churchyard selling relics, while Elfic the Jester gave his first performance in the Orchard.

The Lyons Corner Tea House run by Chris and Mary Marsham was open, as was the Wartime Dairy run by Carol Theobald when the strolling Shakespeare Players arrived in the Orchard. Janet Power and the talented Lustleigh Drama Group rehearsed their own

arrangement of scenes from *A Midsummer Night's Dream* and later performed as a travelling orchestra and the Greenwood Dancers.

The Lustleigh Society had opened the Old Vestry for a historical display; games were being played in the Orchard when the Town Crier, Dave Wills, announced that the official opening of the 'Cleavage Alehouse' would take place. Carolyn Seaward unveiled the 'Cleavage Inn' sign to great applause and merriment, and with that, the party really took off.

The Children's Party, organised by Bev Harman, had started in the Village Hall with face-painting, a treasure hunt and a Punch and Judy show taking place when suddenly a team of Morris Dancers arrived in full regalia – from America. Apparently they had landed at Heathrow at 4.00a.m. and, on hearing that a party was happening, decided to join in. With a barbecue taking place in the Orchard and a hog roast in the Cleavage, events continued to take place throughout the afternoon with the Lustleigh Drama Group and the Pierrot Troupe continuing their performances.

As afternoon turned into evening the stalls packed up and the crowds disappeared, the vintage cars drove away together with the wartime vehicles and who can forget the sight of the steam traction engine, having warmed up by going forwards and back in front of the 'Cleavage', finally seeming to make up its mind and with much tooting of whistles disappearing out of the village? Sadly, the Evening Charity Ball, which Barry Goff and Amanda Harris had worked so hard for, had to be postponed, so, as the evening wore on the barbecue was transported to the Cleavage where, with the church floodlit and providing a beautiful background, the party carried on.

The next day saw the start of tidying up and the return to their owners of all the equipment and implements that had been lent. It was to be some six months later before the final implement (a chaff cutter) was returned.

With the 'Big Event' over the question of 'what next?' arose. This was easy to answer, with a sizeable proportion of parishioners debating as to which New Year was the 'correct' New Year, a special New Year's Eve 2000 was planned.

But first, the Lustleigh Show (the millennium edition) kicked off on Saturday 26 August with an outstanding 'Evening Bash' featuring music by 'Scratch' (the local village band), Ted Malloy's 'Postround Epic' and the 'Village Hall People' performing a 'surprise dance', excerpts of which are on the millennium video.

The main part of Lustleigh Show, held on the August bank holiday Monday, was an outstanding success. With over 3000 people attending and more than 800 cars accommodated, this proved to be a record year for the show. During the year some £5000 was to be donated by the committee to various

Carolyn Seaward unveils the thatched alehouse, the Cleavage Arms,
ably and willingly assisted by Town Crier Dave Wills.

village groups including the Village Hall, Lustleigh Playgroup, Lustleigh Parish Council for playground equipment, and the Cricket Club amongst others.

On 31 December 2000 a large crowd gathered in the Cleave, with the kind permission of Alison Perring, for the start of the evening's entertainment where Don Badger was set to show, for the first time, the millennium video, Don Badger's candid record of some of the events that took place in the village during the year and which starred Emma Wills as the May Queen with a full supporting cast of the children of Lustleigh, the Millennium Fayre and excerpts from the Lustleigh Show Evening Bash. Following the video an even larger crowd now gathered in the Cricket Field, with the kind permission of Ian and Chris Caston, where Dave Wills and his team of helpers were primed to start, despite appalling weather which at one time threatened to flood the field, what was to be the biggest and the best firework display Lustleigh had ever seen. A procession to the church, led and entertained by Jean Hart and her bagpipes then followed, where, with the kind permission of the Parochial Church Council, Anna Robertson had organised a spectacular celebration of music, hymns and readings during which the weather now miraculously cleared in time for the serving of mulled wine on the Church Steps by Peter Milligan and Cheryl Van de Selm.

The 'Grand Raffle' was drawn at the Cleave with the 1st prize of a £30 hamper from the Dairy going to Jean Ross. The proceeds of the 'Grand Raffle' were £280, which, together with any remaining millennium funds, would be split between the Village Hall, Lustleigh Playgroup and the Parochial Church Council.

Floodlighting of the church and the cricket field by Bill Jackson made it possible for Jean to again lead the way to the Cricket Field for the welcoming in of 2001 highlighted by 12 rockets, donated by Alison, and set off from Brookside lawn with the kind permission of Judy Claxton. At one minute past midnight on 1 January 2001 the 2nd Millennium (ad-hoc) Committee disbanded itself having concluded (thankfully) that their efforts were no longer required. Copies of the millennium minutes, Midsummer's Day programme and the millennium video, together with other items, have been placed in the Lustleigh Archives Room where it is hoped that the 3rd Millennium (ad-hoc) Committee will consult them.

Finally, mention must be made of the following persons, in no particular order, without whom none of the events could have taken place: Don Badger, Alison Perring, Patrick Barker, Justin Amery, Bev Harman, Sarah Vantreen, Hilary Gould, Mike Ploog, Amanda Harris, Erica Read, Jenny Webb, Tim Hall, Molly Amery, Carolina Hobbs, Carol Theobald, Peter Milligan, Cheryl Van de Selm, Sandy French, Teresa Bavin, William Bavin, Hugh Gould, Henry Reddaway, Dave Wills, Barry Goff, Carol Smith, Phil Smith, Linda Davies, Carolyn Seaward, Anna Robertson, Will Carnell, David Connell, Ian Caston, Carol Theobald, Bill Jackson, Julia Vittle and Janette Brown.

SUBSCRIBERS

J. D. and H. M. Anderson, Lustleigh, Devon
Eric and Iris Ash, Starparke, Lustleigh, Devon
The Backus family, Lustleigh, Devon
Mrs Margaret Ball (née Olding), Christow, Devon
P. L. and A. J. Barker, Lustleigh, Devon
Vivyan and Val. Bates, Lustleigh, Devon
Sonia Baudouy, Lustleigh, Devon
John and Jane Bean, Eastwrey Barton,
    Lustleigh, Devon
Bill and Anne Beaumont, Lustleigh, Devon
Betty Beer, Crediton, Devon
C. Belam, Ludgate, West Buckfastleigh, Devon
J. D. and C. J. Bewsher
Mr and Mrs Elliot A. Bialick, Lustleigh, Devon
Anita Billington, Bovey Tracey, Devon
Jon Billington, Los Angeles, California
Charles Bowden, Brampton Cottage,
    Lustleigh, Devon
Brian and Zöe Bowman
Eric Braham, Lustleigh, Devon
Master Benjamin Albert Bryant, Lustleigh, Devon
Burgoyne and Haines families, North Harton
K. J. Burrow, Bucks Cross, Devon
Gillian and Ralph Burwood, Guildford
The Carrolls, Bridge Park, Lustleigh, Devon
Caroline Checkley, Milan
Francis Chudley, Bovey Travey, Devon
Judy Claxton, Lustleigh, Devon
Eric and Sue Clutton, Bovey Tracey, Devon
Doug and Fran Cooper, Lustleigh, Devon
Jeff and Jane Cushman, Lustleigh, Devon
Barbara M. Cutts, formerly of Lustleigh, Devon
The Dale family, Lustleigh, Devon
Michael M. Davies, Lustleigh, Devon
Terry and Sue Davy, Lustleigh, Devon
Rosemary Deacon
Jerry Diplock, Lustleigh, Devon
Robert Douglas
John and Grace Dray, Lustleigh, Devon
East Dartmoor Baptist Church, Lustleigh, Devon
Brian, Kate, Joss and Leah Edwards,
    Starmead, Lustleigh, Devon
Joan Ellis, Lustleigh, Devon
Mr R. W. Evans, Boscombe, Dorset
Doris F. Farlow, Lustleigh, Devon
Richard, Rosalind and Oliver Field,
    Plymouth, Devon
Brian S. Folley, Lower Harton Farm,
    Lustleigh, Devon
Edna Franklin, Brampton Cottage, Lustleigh, Devon
Jennifer Garnsey (née Wyatt), Bideford, Devon
K. J. Germon, ex Lustleigh/now Bovey Tracey, Devon
Douglas J. Germon, Bovey Tracey, Devon
B. R. and I. Gibson, South Harton Farm,
    Lustleigh, Devon

Jennifer M. Gould, Lustleigh, Devon
Miss M. E. Gould, Lustleigh, Devon
Hugh Gould, Lustleigh, Devon
Jean I. Green, formerly of Lustleigh, Devon
Tim Hall, Moretonhampstead, Devon
Stuart and Margery Hands, Bickington, Devon
William Hart, Lower Knowle, Lustleigh, Devon
Andrew and Kelly Anne Harvey,
    Knowle House Cottage, Lustleigh, Devon
Ann and Roger Harvey, Knowle House,
    Lustleigh, Devon
George Harvey, Liverton, Devon
The Heather Family, Lustleigh, Devon
Michael Hobbs, Bonwycks, Lustleigh, Devon
Simon Hopwood, Bovey Tracey, Devon
Kim Hopwood, Mortonhampstead, Devon
Peter Howarth, Moorview, Lustleigh, Devon
Mrs Veronica D. Hughes, Lustleigh, Devon
Mrs Celia Hulme, Godalming, Surrey
Bernard and Barbara Igra
Professors Sue and Les Iversen
Revd Kenneth E. Jackson
Vicky and William Jackson, Lustleigh, Devon
Richard Jacoby, Lustleigh, Devon
Drs A. and S. James, Lustleigh, Devon
Alan and Jillian Jeffs, Lustleigh, Devon
J. Audrey Jenkins, Lustleigh, Devon
David and Pam Jervois, Bovey Tracey, Devon
Mrs Ann Jones and Miss P. Roberts, Lustleigh, Devon
Mr and Mrs J. B. Jowitt, Exmouth, Devon
Frau E. C. Kaps, Berlin
Harold and Gladys Kennett, Lustleigh, Devon
Julian Kerven (born 1964), at Parklands,
    Lustleigh, Devon
Colin C. Kilvington, Stoke Plymouth, Devon
Maggie and John King, Lustleigh, Devon
Michael and Margaret Kingham, Dawlish, Devon
Mrs D. A. A. Kinloch, Emsworth, Hampshire
Renee Larcombe, Lustleigh, Devon
Miss J. Lee, Tavistock, Devon
Jeanette and Terry, Justin, and Oliver Lee,
    and Tonya Howell, Lustleigh
Revd Bob and Mary Leigh, Bournemouth, Dorset
Trevor and Alison Linnecar,
    Easton Cottage, Lustleigh, Devon
John and Joan Lloyd, Lustleigh, Devon
Royston and Maureen Lloyd-Baker, Lustleigh, Devon
Brian and Veryan Lundin, Log Hut, Lustleigh, Devon
Daphne Madge (née Knight), Exeter, Devon
James Manners-Chapman, Lustleigh, Devon
Wendy Manners-Chapman, Lustleigh, Devon
Mary J. Marsham, Lustleigh, Devon
The Mason family, Hampshire
Ian McKinlay, Lustleigh, Devon
Ruth M. McRink, Lustleigh, Devon

Christina and Tom Moore, Lustleigh, Devon
Dave Morecombe, Melksham, Wilts.
Lionel and Elizabeth Morecombe, Fairford, Glos.
Mrs Jillian Morgan, Shoreham, Kent
Esau and Nora Moss, Axminster, Devon
Mrs P. M. Nattrass, Basingstoke
Mr N. J. Osborne, Westbury, Wiltshire
J. A. Palmer, Lustleigh, Devon
John and Sheila Peacock, Lustleigh, Devon
Alicia and Neil Peperell
David and Rosemary Perrett, Wincanton, Somerset
Mr and Mrs R. M. Perry, Plymouth, Devon
Freda and Gordon Pike, Ex Lustleigh
Cyril and Joan Plant, Telford, Shropshire
John W. Pollard, Bovey Tracey, Devon
T. Pool, Ilsington, Devon
Raymond Powell, Brampton Cottage,
   Lustleigh, Devon
Mrs Jennie Powys-Lybbe, Lustleigh, Devon
Audrey Prizeman, Plymouth, Devon
Alec N. E. Prowse, Heatree Copse, Manaton, Devon
Mr and Mrs D. W. Puttick, Eastbourne, East Sussex
Mr and Mrs D. Quicke, Lustleigh, Devon
Annie Reddaway, Lustleigh, Devon
Tom Reddaway, Lustleigh, Devon
Mr Peter A. Reynolds, Bovey Tracey, Devon
Ken Rickard, Lydford, Devon
Nancy M. Roach, Lustleigh, Devon
Hilary Roberts and Desmond Rooney,
   Lustleigh, Devon
Tim and Anna Robertson, Mapstone,
   Lustleigh, Devon
Mr and Mrs Rolfe, Lower Dimson, Cornwall
Mr and Mrs Rolfe, Tamerton Foliot, Plymouth, Devon
Jean Ross
Janet A. Rowe, Lustleigh, Devon
Sharon and Nigel Rowland, Wimborne, Dorset
Michael T. G. Rwoe, Lustleigh, Devon
Richard Sheen, Doncaster

Rosemary Skinner, Lustleigh, Devon
Mrs Jean Smeeth (née Wills), Hitchin, Herts.
Eric and Jill Smith, Lustleigh, Devon
Carol and Philip Smith, Gate House,
   Lustleigh, Devon
Marjorie Smith (née Germon), Lustleigh, Devon
Peggy and John Sparks, Lustleigh, Devon
W. H. and N. E. Squires, Lustleigh, Devon
Colin and Millie Squires, Yelland, Devon
Raymond Squires, St Mary, Paignton, Devon
Gp Capt. and Mrs J. A. Stocker
Allan and Beth Storey
Fiona E. Sutcliffe Maynard
David and Rita Swindells, Lustleigh, Devon
Jeane Taylor, Long Tor, Lustleigh, Devon
Carol Theobald, Aylesbury, Bucks.
Sarah and Stephen Vantreen, Thomas,
   Edward, Charlotte and William, Lustleigh
Sue Viccars, Moretonhampstead, Devon
Edward St J. Vittle, Lustleigh, Devon
Nicholas D. Vittle, Lustleigh, Devon
Mr G. Waldron, Plymouth, Devon
John F. W. Walling, Newton Abbot, Devon
Nick Walter, Chudleigh, Devon
Alan and Sheila Watson, Exeter
Philip Weller, Fareham, Hants.
Bob and Jeanie White
Hilary Whitecross (née Knight), Plymouth, Devon
Dick Wills, Narracombe Farm, Ilsington, Devon
Mr D. Eric Wills, Lustleigh, Devon
Carl, Diane and Alice Wills, Manaton, Devon
Mrs S. E. and Miss K. E. Wollen, Lustleigh, Devon
Robert and Helen Wood, Lustleigh, Devon
Michael Wood, Henley
Andrew Wood, Croydon, Surrey
Courtney and Irene Wright, Lustleigh, Devon
Shaun Wright, Lustleigh, Devon
Mike Wright, Lustleigh, Devon
Steve Wright, Lustleigh, Devon

Carpenters take a rest outside Hall House, c.1920.

Jack Horrell in 1952. David Price (who now lives in Godalming) writes: 'The postman was my wife's grandfather, Mr John Horrell, known to all as Jack. In his last years he lived in one of the Brookfield cottages, but when he first came to Lustleigh he lived and worked a smallholding at Lower Combe.

Another much-valued postman, Brian Roach, pictured beside the Mill Leat in 1985. Lustleigh postmen need to have an encyclopaedic knowledge of the village for there are no street names or numbers!

ALSO AVAILABLE IN
THE SERIES

The Book of Addiscombe • Various
Book of Bampton • Caroline Seward
Book of Bickington • Stuart Hands
Blandford Forum: A Millennium Portrait • Various
The Book of Brixham • Frank Pearce
The Parish Book of Cerne Abbas • Vale & Vale
The Book of Chittlehampton • Various
The Book of Constantine • Moore & Trethowan
The Book of Cornwood and Lutton • Various
The Book of Creech St Michael • June Small
The Book of Cullompton • Various
The Book of Dawlish • Frank Pearce
The Ellacombe Book • Sydney R. Langmead
The Book of Grampound with Creed • Bane & Oliver
The Book of Hayling Island and Langstone • Rogers
The Book of Helston • Jenkin with Carter
The Book of Hemyock • Clist & Dracott
The Book of High Bickington • Avril Stone
The Book of Ilsington • Dick Wills
The Book of Lamerton • Ann Cole and Friends
Lanner, A Cornish Mining Parish • Scharron Schwartz
& Roger Parker
The Book of Loddiswell • Various
The Book of Manaton • Various
The Book of Meavy • Pauline Hemery
The Book of Morchard Bishop • Jeff Kingaby
The Book of Minehead with Alcombe • Binding & Stevens
The Book of North Newton • Robins & Robins
The Book of Paignton • Frank Pearce
The Book of Pimperne • Compiled by Jean Coull
The Book of Plymtree • Tony Eames
The Book of Porlock • Denis Corner
Postbridge – The Heart of Dartmoor • Reg Bellamy
The Book of Priddy • Various
The Book of Rattery • Various
The Book of Silverton • Various
The Book of South Stoke • Various
South Tawton and South Zeal with Sticklepath • Roy and
Ursula Radford
*The Book of Sparkwell with Hemerdon
& Lee Mill* • Pam James
The Book of Stithians • Various
The Book of Swanage • Rodney Legg
The Book of Torbay • Frank Pearce
Uncle Tom Cobley and All: Widecombe-in-the-Moor •
Stephen Woods
The Book of Watchet • Compiled by David Banks
The Book of West Huntspill • Various
Widecombe-in-the-Moor • Stephen Woods
The Book of Williton • Michael Williams
Woodbury: The Twentieth Century Revisited • Roger Stokes
The Book of Woolmer Green • Various

SOME OF THE MANY
FORTHCOMING TITLES

The Book of Addiscombe, Vol. II • Various
The Book of Barnstaple • Avril Stone
The Book of Bridestowe • R. Cann
The Book of Buckland Monochorum • Hemery
The Book of Carshalton • Stella Wilks
The Book of Chagford • Ian Rice
*The Book of Chittlehamholt with
Warkleigh & Satterleigh* • Richard Lethbridge
The Book of Colney Heath • Bryan Lilley
The Book of Down St Mary • Various
*The Book of Dulverton
with Brushford, Bury & Exebridge* • Various
The Book of Dunster • Hilary Binding
The Book of Hurn • Margaret Phipps
The Book of Lulworth • Rodney Legg
The Book of Markyate • Richard Hogg
The Book of Mawnan Smith • Various
The Book of Newdigate • John Callcut
The Book of Newton Abbot • Ian Rice
The Book of North Tawton • Various
The Book of Northlew with Ashbury • Various
The Book of Peter Tavy • Various
The Book of Publow with Pensford • Various
*The Book of Sampford Courtenay
with Honeychurch* • Stephanie Pouya
The Book of Staverton • Pete Lavis
The Book of Studland • Rodney Legg
The Book of Wythall • Val Lewis

For details of any of the above titles or if you are interested in writing your own community history, please contact: Community Histories Editor, Halsgrove House, Lower Moor Way, Tiverton Business Park, Tiverton, Devon EX16 6SS, England, e-mail: sales@halsgrove.com If you are particularly interested in any of the images in this volume, it may be possible to supply a copy. Please telephone 01884 243242 for details.

In order to include as many historic photographs as possible in this volume, a printed index is not included. However, the Community Histories are currently being indexed by Genuki. For further information and indexes to volumes in the series, please visit:
http://www.cs.ncl.ac.uk/genuki/DEV/indexingproject.html